THE STRATEGIC MARKETING PLANNING WORKBOOK

FROM

Written and Edited by:

Jose Palomino | Rachel Stephan Simko | Gillian Chick | Lauren Sell

CODY ROCK PRESS  PHILADELPHIA

To activate your Accelerator™ Online subscription forward your order confirmation email to: accelerator@valueprop.com

Inquiries should be directed to:

Cody Rock Press

info@codyrockpress.com

Printed in the United States of America

First Edition

ISBN 978-0-9819126-2-2

Book Design by Lauren Sell

TABLE OF CONTENTS

FlightPlan

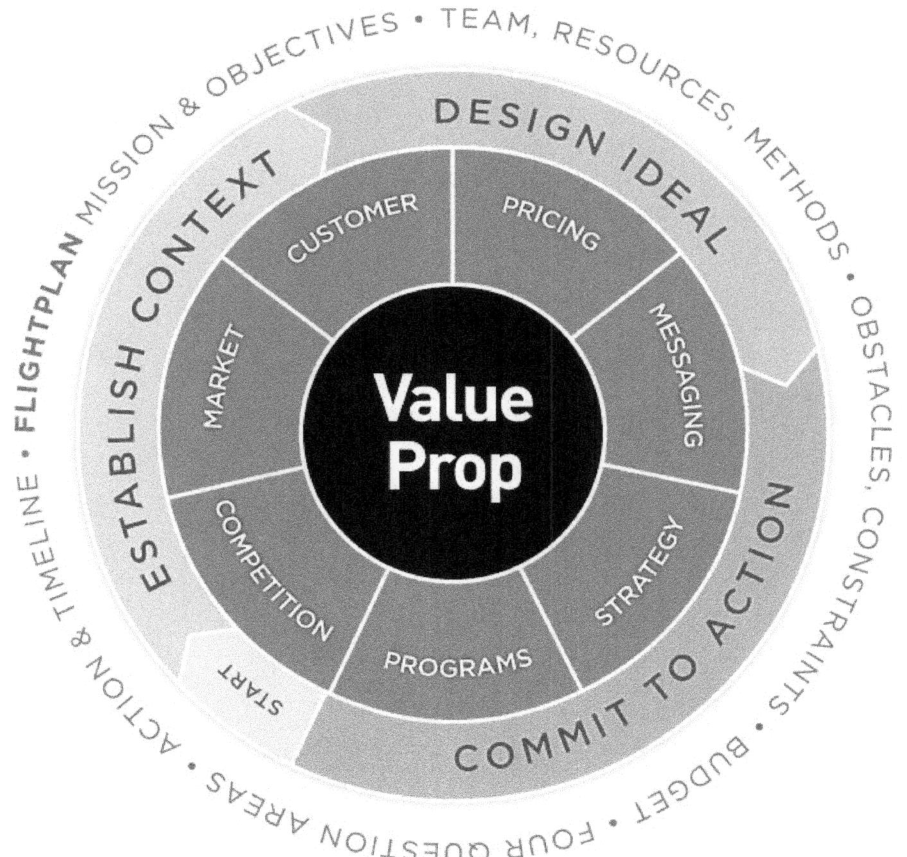
FLIGHTPLAN • MISSION & OBJECTIVES • TEAM, RESOURCES, METHODS • OBSTACLES, CONSTRAINTS • BUDGET • FOUR QUESTION AREAS • ACTION & TIMELINE •
ESTABLISH CONTEXT
DESIGN IDEAL
COMMIT TO ACTION
START
CUSTOMER
PRICING
MESSAGING
STRATEGY
PROGRAMS
COMPETITION
MARKET
Value Prop

What is a FlightPlan?

QC: 3003

The FlightPlan provides the **project framework** for the strategy, positioning, branding, channels, pricing and all the other moving parts of your product/service launch.

In aviation, a **flight plan** documents the intention of the aircraft operator, prior to flight. In the early days, it merely listed the point of departure, the point of arrival, and the intended route of flight in between. It also included a physical description of the aircraft, and contact information for if the aircraft failed to show up at the intended destination. Over time, as airspace saturation began to occur, requirements were added to the flight plan to enable ground controllers to manage traffic. As radio communication became more common, it became standard procedure to update changes in flight plan parameters such as TAS, altitude, and time estimates via radio while en route.

The FlightPlan articulates the key real-world elements that make go-to-market strategies "happen."

According to former Navy Captain and major airline pilot, Scott Davies, before a commercial airliner is allowed to take off, it must file a flight plan.

A flight plan is the official report that aircraft operators file with controlling aviation authorities, documenting their intended route and other parameters for the flight. Prior to the advent of flight tracking and navigational technologies such as radios, radar, and GPS, there needed to be some record of intended flight operation.

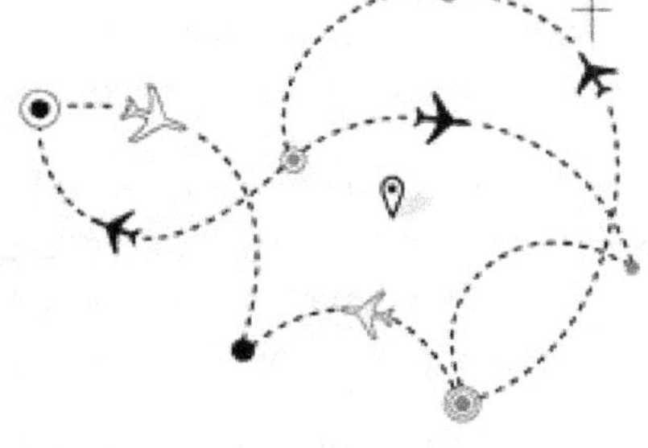

Throughout the decades of changes in air traffic monitoring, the flight plan has continued to serve as the basic document for filing the initial intentions of the aircraft operator prior to flight. This way, in the event of lost radio or radar contact, there remains a base plan that pilots and controllers can refer to in order to anticipate the continued conduct of the flight.

These regulations allow thousands of planes to fly every day – largely without incidence.

The essence of these rules and process can be summarized as readiness, clarity, and direction – all elements of the Go-To-Market FlightPlan.

What does the FlightPlan™ do for Go-To-Market?

Alice: *I was just wondering if you could help me find my way.*

Cheshire Cat: *Well that depends on where you want to get to.*

Alice: *Oh, it really doesn't matter, as long as…*

Cheshire Cat: *Then it really doesn't matter which way you go.*

– Alice in Wonderland

- Do you know where your company is going?
- Have you articulated the key benchmarks for your firm's success in the marketplace?
- Are you aware of the key resources and tools that will powerfully transfer your message to the mind of your target customer?
- Does your organization have an actionable and accountable timeline?

Picture a Godiva™ chocolate treat – delicious, smooth-textured, and delivering a powerful taste sensation.

Now picture the wrapper, silver and gold, with a delicate non-stick tissue on the inside – perfectly preserving and delivering these special confections as intended.

In the same way, the Value Prop Method has two major pieces – a "tasty core" – messaging and strategic plan **and** a "wrapper" – a process for tracking and driving the "traction" elements of your go to market program. Strategy, positioning, brand, channels, pricing and all the other moving parts of your program have to be put into operation by people, using resources and committing to specific actions – and the FlightPlan guides that activity

According to frequent Harvard Business Review contributor, Michael Mankins, "despite the enormous time and energy that goes into strategy development at most companies, many have little to show for the effort. Our research suggests that companies on average deliver only 63% of the financial performance their strategies promise." [1]

The FlightPlan articulates the key real-world elements that make go-to-market strategies "happen."

In a holistic manner, it details the measurable objectives, actions, and other planning elements needed for carrying out the strategy you've formed so far. In the end, the FlightPlan will allow you to state the functional elements of your go-to-market program crisply, including key objectives, key dates and other action-oriented or facilitating elements.

Each of the FlightPlan elements are developed in two phases.

Initially, "sketch in" the FlightPlan with real-time notes during the development of your overall go-to-market plan and program. We call this core piece (the tasty chocolate of messaging, strategy and analysis) the Acceleration Framework and will describe in detail later.

Later, you will revise an "official" Version 1.0 during some structured discussion time, to give you a game plan to carry out your firm's go-to-market strategy.

The FlightPlan provides a standard "action language" for all elements of your go-to-market program, whether they are strategic, tactical or informational. The key elements of the FlightPlan that will bring your go-to-market strategy to life include:

- Mission
- Objectives
- Obstacles
- Timeline
- Budget
- Action
- Resources & Tools
- The Four Question Areas

QC: 3003

[1] Mankins, Michael C. and Richard Steele. "Turning Great Strategy into Great Performance." *Harvard Business Review* July – August 2005.

FlightPlan

- Mission
  - Company Mission
  - Product/Service Mission
  - Mission Alignment

ValuePropInteractive

QC: 414

NOTES:

FlightPlan

- Objectives
  - Strategic Objectives
  - Tactical Objectives
  - Specific, measurable, time-bound

ValuePropInteractive

QC: 416

NOTES:

FlightPlan

- Team
  - Core Team
  - Close Advisors
  - Customer Advisors
  - Professional Advisors

ValuePropInteractive

QC: 127

NOTES:

FlightPlan

- Resources
  - Brand
  - IP/Methodology
  - People/Skills
  - Budget

ValuePropInteractive

QC: 3791

NOTES:

FlightPlan

- **Obstacles** are the "boulders in the path" that, with a little creativity and elbow grease, you can usually overcome.
- **Constraints** are the finite boundaries you have to work within.

ValuePropInteractive

QC: 419

NOTES:

FlightPlan

- Budget

ValuePropInteractive

QC: 421

NOTES:

FlightPlan

- Action/Timeline
  - Marketplace Timeline
  - Internal Timeline
  - Action Plan

ValuePropInteractive

QC: 444

NOTES:

FlightPlan

- Four Question Areas
  - Issues to be resolved
  - Decisions to be made
  - Information gaps
  - Know-how/expertise gaps

ValuePropInteractive

QC: 423

NOTES:

FlightPlan Readiness Assessment

The **FlightPlan Readiness Assessment** enables your team to assess where they think the team stands in terms of adopting and using the FlightPlan to manage this initiative to a successful launch.

Mark the statements you agree with in the open box to the right:

#	QUESTION	+	–
1	We work with very structured Project Plans.		
2	Everyone on the team is crystal clear on our Objectives.		
3	We have crisply defined the success metrics (financial, market share, etc.) for this project.		
4	Team members' roles and responsibilities are not clearly defined.		
5	We process issues and decisions very well.		
6	We do not have anyone outside our group helping us.		
7	We understand our burn rate (or for larger companies, budget) and how much time we have left.		
8	We don't really have a clear idea as to what has to get done, by whom, and when?		
	Count the checks in each column:		
	Subtract the total in the "–" column from the total in the "+" column to calculate your FlightPlan Readiness Score:		

QC: 3174

The Four Question Areas introduced in the FlightPlan arise throughout the life of your project. Use them as a framework to identify and sort through any questions or situations that come up which may slow your progress toward your Go-to-Market goals. (Many will fit into more than one quadrant, or move from one to the next as you work through them.)

QC: 423

Issues to be resolved:	Decisions to be made:
Information Gaps to be filled:	**Know-How Gaps to be filled:**

FlightPlan Worksheet

QC: 4128

The FlightPlan is an overall Project Management Framework for developing a strategic and actionable marketing program.

Mission

QC: 414

Your mission is the end-goal, so measure everything you do against it.

What is your company's overarching mission? Why are you in business?

What is the mission or purpose for this initiative? Why does your offering exist?

How tightly are your company's mission and your product's mission aligned?

Objectives

QC: 416

Keep objectives clear and specific. Use time-bound targets that are as measurable as possible. Consider both strategic objectives (the company's high-level corporate strategy, financial goals, and market impact goals), as well as more immediately tangible tactical objectives (reflecting the critical areas of project management, overall efficiency, and time management).

What are your high-level Strategic Objectives?

What are some of your specific Tactical Objectives?

What are the Revenue/Unit Sales Goals for this initiative?

(e.g., "1000 Units sold in Q1, 1500 in Q2, 6000 for year, with a revenue of $5M and margins of 25%.")

Team

QC: 127

Who is on your team? Take inventory of both your immediate organization, and the larger circle of professionals around you.

Core Team:

Close Advisors:

Customer Advisors:

Professional Advisors:

Resources

QC: 3791

What resources do you have at your disposal? Consider your brand, intellectual property, methodology, skills of those on your team, and of course your budget.

What resources do we have available to us?

What budget do we have? What budget do we still need to find?

The budget should reflect the best and most practical, high-impact methods for connecting your product's message to your target customer. Line items are typically advertising, public relations, promotional items, events (exhibit, sponsor, and attend), as well as personnel costs to support all of these.

QC: 421

Obstacles

QC: 419

Obstacles are the "boulders in the path" that, with a little creativity and elbow grease, you can usually overcome.

	OBSTACLE	RESOLUTION
1		
2		
3		
4		
5		

Constraints

QC: 419

Constraints are the finite boundaries you have to work within.

	CONSTRAINT	RESOLUTION
1		
2		
3		
4		
5		

Action/Timeline

QC: 444

The Timeline and Action Plan reflect two environments: the external marketplace, and your internal environment.

Marketplace Timeline

What's happening in your marketplace? In what timeframe do you expect it to happen? How much of an impact will it have on your go-to-market success?

Consider the following questions as you fill in the chart:

- What are the key expectations and needs of your target/prototypical customer?
- When will competitors likely respond to your product offering?
- What are the current technology trends in the marketplace, and how can we source and engineer solutions that reflect these trends?
- Are there regulatory issues that will affect our firm's go-to-market process?
- What progress are our competitors making?

IMPACT	TIMEFRAME			
	30 DAYS	6 MONTHS	1 YEAR	3 YEARS
High				
Medium-High				
Medium-Low				
Low				

Internal Timeline

QC: 444

With that awareness of what's going on in your marketplace in the coming months and years, what are you as a company planning to do in those same timeframes? What will the impact be on your go-to-market success?

Incorporate the following key time-based elements or schedules:

- Product Development
- Product Launch
- Sales Year (calendar or fiscal)
- VC or Funding Stakeholder Target
- Product Sales Training
- Other Strategic Dates

IMPACT	TIMEFRAME			
	30 DAYS	6 MONTHS	1 YEAR	3 YEARS
High				
Medium-High				
Medium-Low				
Low				

Action Plan

Take the timeline down to a more granular level of detail, breaking down what needs to happen in order meet key dates and accomplish your objectives. It could be a simple task list detailing assignments (including who's responsible and deadlines), or you may require dedicated project management software for larger/more complex initiatives. Use the Action Items feature Accelerator™ to assign key tasks to your project team.

Four Question Areas

QC: 423

First, identify major issues as they surface, noting where "gaps" still exist. Then, break down those issues into key decisions that need to be made while going to market. Finally, what information and expertise is needed to execute the FlightPlan? How will you fill these gaps? (Revisit the Four Question Areas after the Assessment in each section.)

What major issues must be faced?

What key decisions must be made?

What information are we missing?

What expertise or "know-how" will we need?

Customer

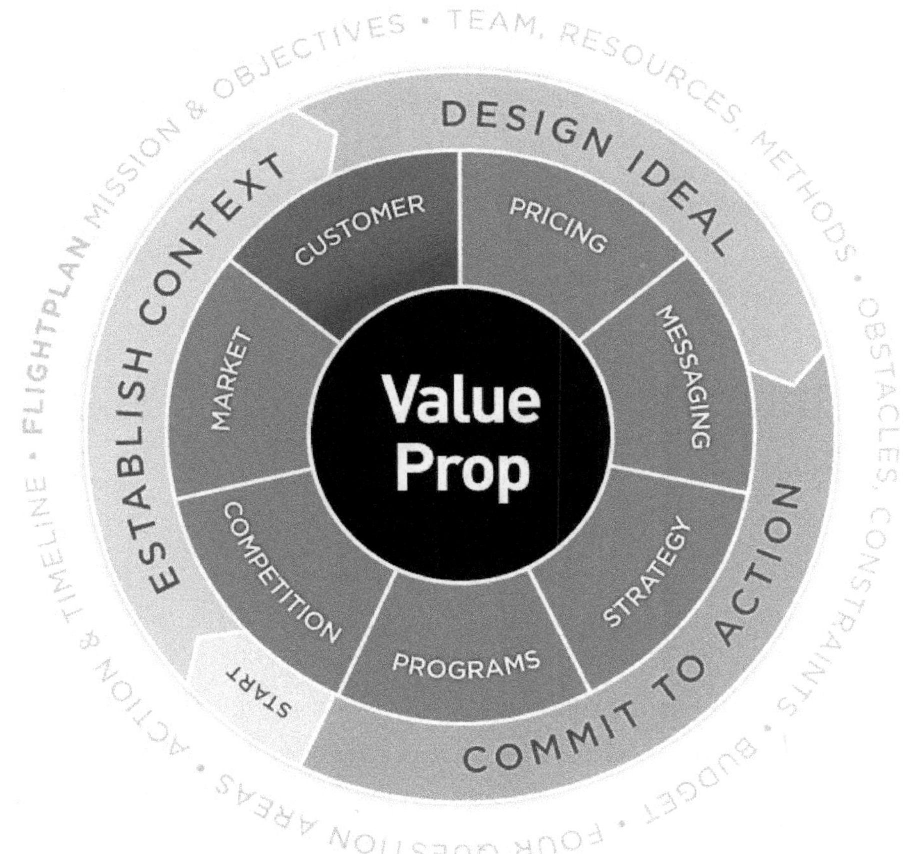
FLIGHTPLAN MISSION & OBJECTIVES • TEAM, RESOURCES, METHODS • OBSTACLES, CONSTRAINTS • BUDGET • FOUR QUESTION AREAS • ACTION & TIMELINE •
ESTABLISH CONTEXT
DESIGN IDEAL
COMMIT TO ACTION
START
CUSTOMER
PRICING
MESSAGING
STRATEGY
PROGRAMS
COMPETITION
MARKET
Value Prop

Targeting Your Ideal Customer QC: 42

- Know your real customer, and focus your attention and programs specifically on them.
- Doing well with the customers you can reach at first will give you traction to expand your reach.

Remember to think about your real customer.

Take the following (somewhat) hypothetical example about a content management software company within a specific industry.

An industry data provider brings them into many of their clients. The data provider sees the content management platform as a way to get their information to their customers more effectively. The software provider has limited access to the end-user. They may not fully grasp that their real customer is the data provider. They may recognize them as a channel – a critical one. Instead of modifying their business model to better serve channel partners, however, they pursue the end-customer – without having established independent access to them.

Either strategy could work if you know who your **real customer** is and focus your attention and programs on them. This means that you have to determine your **real** and **best** customer, and these are not necessarily the same thing.

Whose problem can we solve?

Look at your target market and customer in the following dimensions: Define your customer by a problem that they have and that you solve. Make a list of your product's attributes, and match them to the needs of that specific customer. Think of it as a table with two columns – product attributes and customer needs.

This is not the same as your I^3 Value Proposition. In this case, you're not describing the actual quality or attractiveness of the attributes (as we would in an I^3 analysis).

Instead, you are simply listing attributes that match your customer's needs – regardless if the attribute is particularly compelling, unique or special in any way. In other words, your offering may not be exceptional in any I^3 dimension, but does **solve a set of problems for a specific group of customers**.

Understanding Your Customer

- Know Thy Customers... are People
- Know Thy Customers' Motivations
- Know Thy Customers' Requirements
- Design Your Real and Best Customer

ValuePropInteractive

QC: 606

NOTES:

Designing Your Ideal Customer

- Access
  - Who do you have experience working with?
  - Appropriate level decision-maker
  - Industry
  - Geography
  - Company size
  - Who are you organized to do business with?

ValuePropInteractive

QC: 5248

NOTES:

Designing Your Ideal Customer

- Ideal Customer
  - Whose problem can you solve best?
  - Who is your customer?
    - Historically
    - Ideally

ValuePropInteractive QC: 42&49

NOTES:

Designing Your Ideal Customer

- Customer Personal Profile
  - Their Objectives
  - Their Problems
  - Their Challenges
  - Their Fears
  - Their Opportunities

ValuePropInteractive

QC: 50

NOTES:

FLIGHTPLAN CUSTOMER MARKET COMPETITION VALUE PROP PRICING MESSAGING STRATEGY PROGRAMS

Aligned Prospects

- Identify the attributes of your current customer base.
- Look for those attributes in other markets or other customer "pools."
- Align to the newer prospects – adjust your messaging and programs.
- Drive new revenue into your company.

ValuePropInteractive QC: 51

NOTES:

FLIGHTPLAN CUSTOMER MARKET COMPETITION VALUE PROP PRICING MESSAGING STRATEGY PROGRAMS

Negatively Aligned Prospects

- All sales are **not** equally beneficial to your company.
- If your messaging isn't aligned with your best offering and the direction you're trying to go, the customers it attracts won't be either.
- Your *current* customers may be holding you back from reaching your *ideal* customers.

ValuePropInteractive QC: 52

NOTES:

Ideal Customer Design Assessment

The Ideal Customer Design Assessment enables your team to assess where they think the team stands in terms of defining and designing your Ideal Customer.

Mark the statements you agree with in the open box to the right:

#	QUESTION	+	–
1	We know who our best customer is.		
2	We have some customers we'd probably be better off not dealing with.		
3	We know what we need to do to get access to the right people in our target companies.		
4	We have a clear understanding as to what makes our best current customers our ideal customer / target market (or why they aren't).		
5	We don't really know as much about our target market as we should.		
6	We consistently leverage our current customers to get new ones.		
7	We understand our strengths and weaknesses in connection with serving our target customer.		
8	We don't really have the staff, resources, and history to impress our target market.		
	Count the checks in each column:		
	Subtract the total in the "–" column from the total in the "+" column to calculate your Customer Assessment Score:		

QC: 3555

The Four Question Areas introduced in the FlightPlan arise throughout the life of your project. Use them as a framework to identify and sort through any questions or situations that come up which may slow your progress toward your Go-to-Market goals. (Many will fit into more than one quadrant, or move from one to the next as you work through them.)

QC: 423

Issues to be resolved:	**Decisions** to be made:
Information Gaps to be filled:	**Know-How Gaps** to be filled:

Ideal Customer Design Worksheet

QC: 4117

Access QC: 5248

If you want to sell to a specific type of company you need to have access to call, talk, and meet with the appropriate level of decision-maker at that organization.

With what type of company / customers do we have the most experience?

What level decision maker can we access?

With whom do we want to do business?

With whom are we best organized to do business?

Do we have the access and experience needed to reach those with whom we want to do business?

	REQUIRED COMPETENCE	STATUS / CURRENT GAP	REQUIRED to CLOSE GAP	COST to CLOSE GAP
Industry:				
Geography:				
Company Size:				
Decision Maker Level:				
Other:				

Your Ideal Customer

QC: 42

The "bull's eye" of your target market – the best to aim for and most valuable to hit – is your ideal customer. Doing well with the customers you can reach at first will give you traction to expand your reach later.

Whose problem can we solve best? Why?

Who is our ideal customer?

(Industry / Geography / Demographic / Psychographic... Be as sharply descriptive as possible.)

This is our ideal customer because:

Customer Personal Profile QC: 50

People – not "organizations" – make business decisions. Know your customer on a human level – their objectives, problems, challenges, fears, and opportunities, and shape your offering and messaging to meet them.

What are our customers' Objectives? QC: 43

What are our customers' Problems? QC: 44

What are our customers' Challenges? QC: 45

What are our customers' Fears? QC: 46

What are our customers' Opportunities? QC: 47

Market

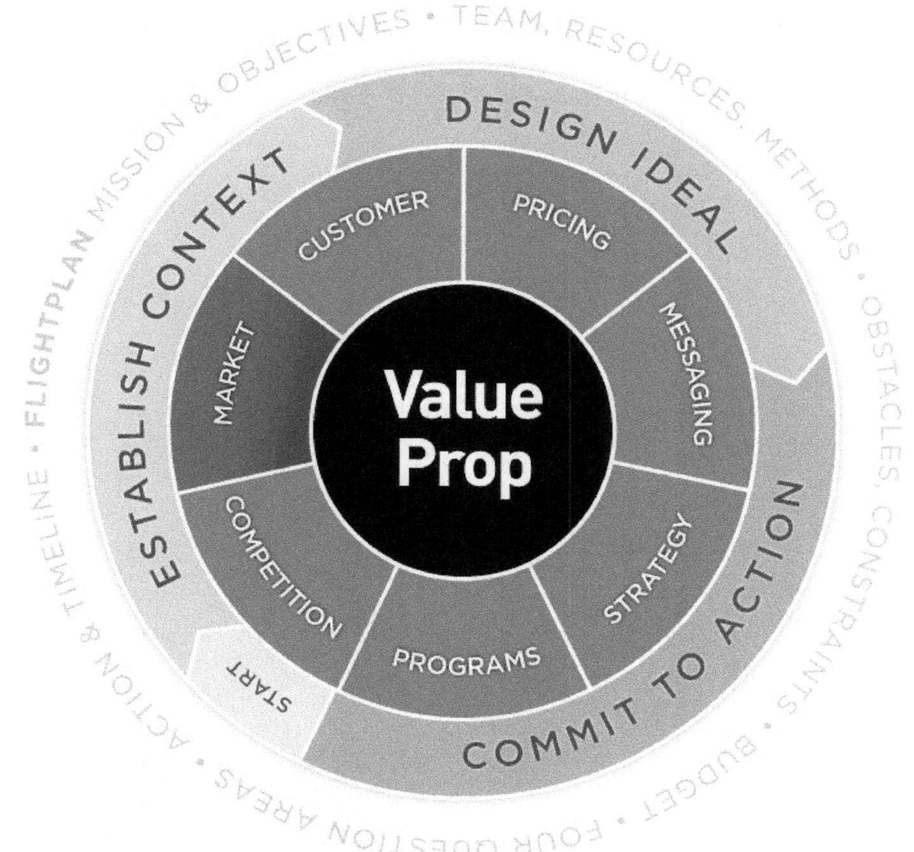
FLIGHTPLAN MISSION & OBJECTIVES • TEAM, RESOURCES, METHODS • OBSTACLES, CONSTRAINTS • BUDGET • FOUR QUESTION AREAS • ACTION & TIMELINE •
ESTABLISH CONTEXT
DESIGN IDEAL
COMMIT TO ACTION
START
CUSTOMER
PRICING
MESSAGING
STRATEGY
PROGRAMS
COMPETITION
MARKET
Value Prop

Identify, Influence, Navigate

QC: 541

- **Identify** marketplace forces that impact your I³ Value Proposition.
- **Influence** the forces that can be influenced, to whatever degree possible.
- **Navigate** through or around the "currents" your company cannot change.

In *Know-How,* Ram Charan zeroes in on the requirement that competent business leaders must be aware of the external environment – the changing factors that determine the future repositioning of the business.

In essence, this is a key concept for business leaders today, due to the much higher rate of business change in a global economy. It is critical that business leaders be aware of the marketplace and societal forces that will shape the success of their businesses. You have to be ahead of the curve and understand what is going on in your chosen market.

Market Dynamics

QC: 543

Market Segment Dynamics examine the entire vertical world of your target industry, and the factors that affect that industry as a whole.

We will look at five of these dynamics – each of which have to identified, influenced, or navigated.

The term "industry" refers to the specific vertical market that your firm plans to engage in its specific go-to-market initiative. Your firm may target several markets, in which case you will need to complete this analysis several times.

Businesses now reside in the world of Sarbanes-Oxley, where heightened regulation likely requires big-ticket buyers to seek far more formal approval than they would have in years past. "Legal fear has become a defining feature of our culture," observes Philip K. Howard, Partner of Covington and Burling, a well known technology industry law firm.

The day and age where a single individual could sign off on a $100,000 purchase order is long gone in most organizations. The Martha Stewart and Enron cases were real and their repercussions have had a ripple effect in all aspects of the broader marketplace. These few but crucial instances in recent history have drastically affected the climate of oversight, checks, and balances in which buyers engage in big-ticket sales. Yet, this represents only a single, generalized example of how buyer behavior will affect your firm's market entry.

The Big Picture

Look at the big picture of your marketplace. There are five primary areas of Market Dynamics to identify, influence, and navigate:

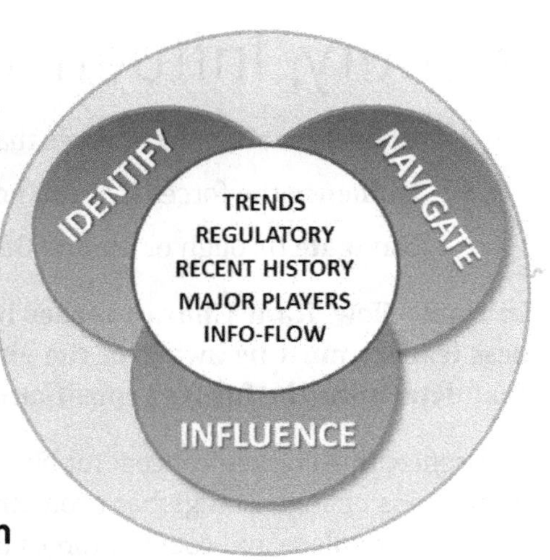

- Trends
- Major Players
- Recent History
- Regulatory Environment
- Information Flow

There are three iterative processes in defining the Marketplace Matrix:

- **Identify:** Articulate key factors and their impact on the I³ Value Proposition.
- **Influence:** What is the firm's ability to influence these factors? How can you influence a specific market factor? To what degree can you influence or change it?
- **Navigate:** If the firm is unable to influence a current condition, what is its ability to navigate around the factor? Should you attempt to influence or navigate?

While it is tempting to dive headfirst into the marketplace and begin selling, the ability to identify, influence, and navigate the Marketplace Matrix will radically affect the success and scope of your go-to-market program. You can acknowledge or ignore Market factors, but the Marketplace Matrix you compete in exists regardless. Much as weather and terrain affect mountain climbers – the Marketplace Matrix is a way of understanding the factors that "are" – the factors that affect your firm's marketing and sales effectiveness in the marketplace.

ACTION:	Identify	Influence	Navigate
KEY QUESTIONS:	What are the key factors? What is their impact on our I³ Value Proposition?	What is our ability to influence these factors? How can we influence a specific market factor? To what degree can we influence or change it?	If we cannot influence a current condition, what is our ability to navigate around the factor? Should we attempt to influence or navigate?

Marketplace Matrix

- The Marketplace Matrix is a way of *understanding your target market.*
- Overlooking crucial outside forces and key changes in your competitive marketplace can be detrimental to your project outcome.
- Understanding Marketplace Matrix elements will increase your ability to better **influence** and **navigate** your marketplace.

ValuePropInteractive QC: 601

NOTES:

FLIGHTPLAN CUSTOMER MARKET COMPETITION VALUE PROP PRICING MESSAGING STRATEGY PROGRAMS

Marketplace Matrix-Factors

- Trends
- Major Players
- Recent History
- Regulatory Environment
- Information Flow

ValuePropInteractive QC: 543

NOTES:

Marketplace Matrix – Key Concepts

- Identify
- Influence
- Navigate

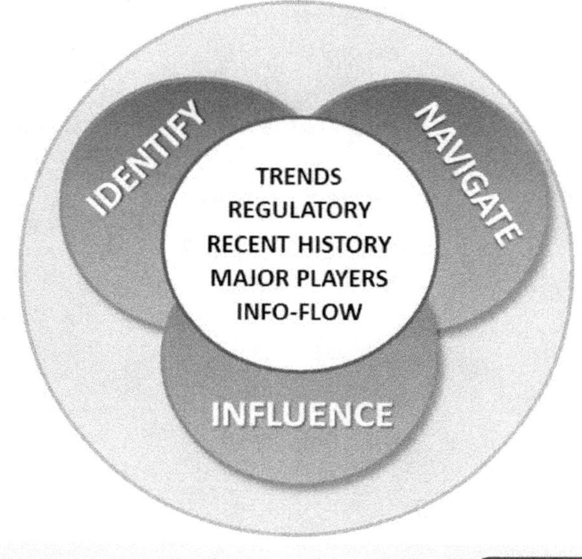

ValuePropInteractive

QC: 541

NOTES:

FLIGHTPLAN | CUSTOMER | MARKET | COMPETITION | VALUE PROP | PRICING | MESSAGING | STRATEGY | PROGRAMS

Marketplace Matrix – Key Questions

ACTION:	*Identify*	*Influence*	*Navigate*
KEY QUESTIONS:	**What are the key factors**? What is their impact on our I^3 Value Proposition?	What is our **ability** to influence these factors? **How** can we **influence** a specific market factor? To what **degree** can we influence or change it?	If we are unable to influence a current condition, what is our ability to **navigate around** the factor? Should we attempt to influence or navigate?

ValuePropInteractive

QC: 541

NOTES:

Company Context

- Industry
- Company
- Capabilities
- Product/Service
- Current Position
- Opportunity

ValuePropInteractive QC: 59

NOTES:

Marketplace Matrix Assessment

The **Marketplace Matrix Assessment** questions are designed to measure your project readiness in knowing your ideal target market and the forces at work within it.

Armed with the concepts from this module your team should be able to pinpoint what the market looks like, how it is changing, what is impacting change and which factors you can influence.

Mark the statements you agree with in the open box to the right:

#	QUESTION	+	−
1	We still need to define our ideal target market.		
2	Our team has a tightly defined sense of our major competitors for our ideal market.		
3	We still need to clearly define the opportunity within our target market.		
4	We have a clear understanding of our ideal market's pressure points and what impacts them.		
5	We know which market elements we can influence and which we cannot.		
6	We have a clear understanding of the regulatory environments we, and our prospects, operate in.		
7	We know which trends are impacting our ideal market right now.		
8	We know exactly what to research next, to better understand our ideal market.		
9	We aren't clear on where exactly we stand in the marketplace, or what opportunity we have in it.		
	Count the checks in each column:		
	Subtract the total in the "–" column from the total in the "+" column to calculate your Marketplace Matrix Score:		

QC: 3553

The Four Question Areas introduced in the FlightPlan arise throughout the life of your project. Use them as a framework to identify and sort through any questions or situations that come up which may slow your progress toward your Go-to-Market goals. (Many will fit into more than one quadrant, or move from one to the next as you work through them.)

QC: 423

Issues to be resolved:	**Decisions** to be made:
Information Gaps to be filled:	**Know-How Gaps** to be filled:

Market Worksheet

QC: 4141

At a high level, describe the Marketplace you will be competing in:

Marketplace Matrix

QC: 541

Identify: What are the key factors and their impact on your I^3 Value Proposition?

Influence: What is the firm's ability to influence these factors?

Navigate: If the firm is unable to influence a current factor, what is your ability to navigate around it?

Trends

QC: 545

Keep an eye on things affecting the industry, and buyer behavior within the industry. Trends may be favorable or challenging, but understanding them will shed light on your current position in the market.

	IDENTIFY	INFLUENCE	NAVIGATE
Trend #1			
Trend #2			
Trend #3			

Major Players

QC: 547

Each industry has major players who are respected and looked to for guidance, both micro and macro. Identify corporations, individuals, competitors, and other vendors who could affect your offering's chance of success.

	IDENTIFY	INFLUENCE	NAVIGATE
Major Player #1			
Major Player #2			
Major Player #3			

Recent History

QC: 549

Examine recent events within your industry. Take into account your company's history in this market, as well as any major market changes.

	IDENTIFY	INFLUENCE	NAVIGATE
Recent Event #1			
Recent Event #2			
Recent Event #3			

Regulatory Environment

QC: 551

Understand the existing legal framework in which your target customers operate. Be aware of the ever-changing regulatory environment and significant causes or issues relevant to your customers.

	IDENTIFY	INFLUENCE	NAVIGATE
Regulatory Factor #1			
Regulatory Factor #2			
Regulatory Factor #3			

Information Flow

QC: 553

Every market segment trusts or seeks its information from specific sources. It may be a niche blog, trade journal, or major newspaper. What are the most important channels for information flow in your market?

	IDENTIFY	INFLUENCE	NAVIGATE
Information Source #1			
Information Source #2			
Information Source #3			

Company Context

QC: 59

Whether you're part of a multi-national Fortune 100 company, or you're an entrepreneurial start-up, understanding some moving parts around your own company is critical to understanding your market.

In what industry do you, as a company, identify yourself? In what industry would your current customers – and more importantly, your prospects – identify you?

This actually has more nuance to it than you might expect. For example, if you sell financial software, are you in Information Technology, or are you in Software? Or are you really a Financial Services player?

QC: 61

Give a more detailed description of your company at present.

Include how long you've been in business, how big your staff is, your relative financial strength, and anything else that helps you really "capture" your company.

QC: 62

What is the product or service that you are offering?

You'll look at this in much more depth later on, but you should be able to convey the "big idea" of "what is it?" in a few descriptive sentences.

QC: 64

What are your current capabilities?

QC: 63

Take inventory of your company's current strengths and abilities – note which are real distinctives and which are merely "table stakes." What capabilities are you lacking?

What is your current position in the market?

QC: 65

To get where you want to go, you have to know where you're starting from. Where does your company stand, presently, in your marketplace?

What is the opportunity for your company and your product or service?

Why are you doing this initiative? What is the prize you think you can gain, that makes the pursuit worthwhile?

QC: 66

Other Relevant Information:

QC: 60

Competition

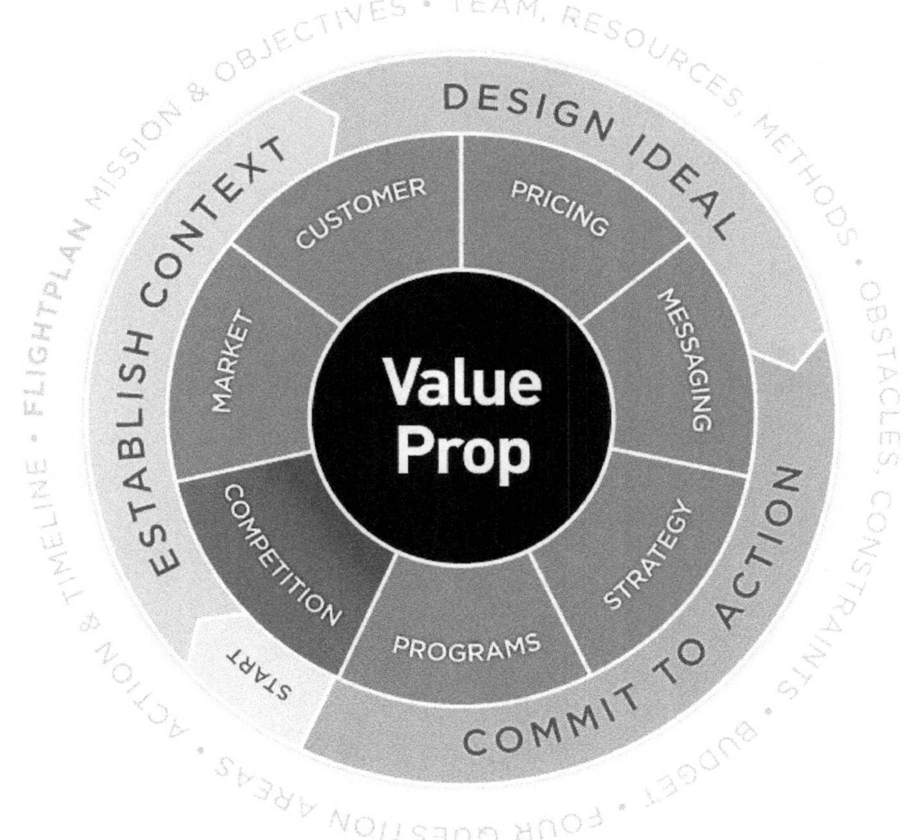

FLIGHTPLAN MISSION & OBJECTIVES • TEAM, RESOURCES, METHODS • OBSTACLES, CONSTRAINTS • BUDGET • FOUR QUESTION AREAS • ACTION & TIMELINE •
ESTABLISH CONTEXT
DESIGN IDEAL
COMMIT TO ACTION
START
CUSTOMER
PRICING
MESSAGING
STRATEGY
PROGRAMS
COMPETITION
MARKET
Value Prop

You're Not Paranoid If...

QC: 3102

...Someone *IS* behind you!

- Examine your target market closely, from different perspectives. What "security measures" do you have to deal with to get through that door?
- Look at the market – and your competition in it – from your prospect's point of view.
- Identify who else is trying to go through the same "door."

"...in the fight for market share, competition is not manifested only in the other players... competitive forces exist that go well beyond the established combatants in a particular industry."

– Dr. Michael E. Porter

Consider these questions:

- Are you *entering* or *changing* a marketplace?
- Does the target customer see your competition the way that you see them?
- What messages are already communicated to your target market?

Picture a wall of infinite doors locked in front of you. From a distance, you determine that each door has multiple locks, secret bolts, and hidden hinges. **This is your marketplace.** It's your choice which door you attempt to open.

Examine the attributes of the door: Is it booby-trapped? Where are the hinges? Does the lock require a key or a combination? By looking at the situation from these varying perspectives you see the situation differently than before.

Now do the same with your marketplace. Look at some of the driving factors in your target market, **from your prospect's point of view.**

How they gather information, who influences them, and what trends and regulatory issues affect them, all contribute to a complex decision framework. This is a framework or playing field, which your marketing and direct sales efforts must identify, influence, or navigate.

Peter Drucker's statement — *"Understand that what is important is what's important to the customer. That's what we all paid for in the last analysis: how does the customer buy, and why?"* – captures the essence of the insight needed by you and your organization.

With this understanding you now stand at the proverbial "door" – looking to turn the key which is now in your possession. Then you realize, "This is too easy. There has to be something more." And there is.

The next step is to glance around and identify the **others** who are trying to squeeze past you and through **your door**. Who is trying to elbow you out of the way, as you're trying to turn the key? Or more graphically, who's trying to hit you over the head with a tire iron while you fish the key out of your pocket?

Competitors, **Alternatives**, and **Disruptors** are three forces that exist within every marketplace – all capable of either keeping you from entering the chosen door, or to push you back out – to make your offering irrelevant to your prospect.

Perhaps you're asking, *"Isn't this where Positioning comes in?"* The answer is yes – and – you need to understand these forces and circle back to your I^3 and positioning work done thus far. Developing an effective go-to-market program is an iterative and holistic process.

QC: 3102

Competition

- Define "Competitors"

QC: 624

NOTES:

Competitive Matrix

- Direct Competitors
- Alternatives
- Disruptors

QC: 624

NOTES:

Avoid Tunnel Vision

Hypothetical Product: Process Mapping Software Competitor, Alternative or Disruptor?						
	Our Key Differentiators	**The Other Company?**	**Feature to Compare**	**Your Advantage**	**Their Advantage**	**Product or Positioning Response**
Competitor	*Our process reduces cycle time by 50%*	*C-Ajax Processing*	*CycleReducer Software*	*Nothing new to buy*	*Reduces cycle time by 60%*	*50% for no new investment vs. 60% with significant dollar outlay*
Alternative		*A-Process redesign*	*Client could revisit their processes and reduce cycle time*	*Plug in process improvement with training support*	*No cost*	*Better results with support*
Disruptor		*D-Trend in client industry is outsourcing this function*	*outsourcing*	*Keep better control of process*	*Reduce cost in long term by going to China*	*Quality control – keep their competitive advantage.*

ValuePropInteractive

QC: 635

NOTES:

FLIGHTPLAN
CUSTOMER
MARKET
COMPETITION
VALUE PROP
PRICING
MESSAGING
STRATEGY
PROGRAMS

Competitive Communications

- Claims
- Symbols
- Messages

ValuePropInteractive

QC: 647

NOTES:

Research is free...

- Talk to your customers and prospects.
- Talk to your sales force.
- The Internet.
- Commission or purchase market research.
- Build relationships with key people within your specific trade press.

ValuePropInteractive

QC: 639

NOTES:

FLIGHTPLAN | CUSTOMER | MARKET | COMPETITION | VALUE PROP | PRICING | MESSAGING | STRATEGY | PROGRAMS

Competitive Communications

- ***Claims*** are **assertions**, typically characterized by a measurable factor.
  - Claims *sound* like statements of fact, whether they are factual or not.
  - For example, "...our switches reduce network latency by 40%..."
- ***Symbols*** are the **pictures** that organizations use to communicate claims and messages.
  - Symbols are more than just logos; symbols are how organizations connect with customers.
  - Vendors often use visual metaphors for speed, power, and efficiency – even in heavy industry or commercial product categories.
- ***Messages*** are the **emotional words** that are communicated in terms of the product's Value Proposition.
  - Particularly in the high-tech world, the message is not only the slogan, but may also include broader details surrounding the product.

ValuePropInteractive QC: 645

NOTES:

Competitive Communications

- What are your competitors?
  - How do theirs stand up to yours?
  - How do theirs hold up against the facts?
  - Are any of those damaging to you?
- Which of yours distinguishes you the most?
- Which might expose your weaknesses?

Simplified Competitive Communications Inventory				
Competitor	**Claims**	**Symbols**	**Messages**	**I^3 Dynamic**
Ajax Processing Services[a]	Lowest Cost Longest history in Legal Vertical	Cash Register blown up Judges Gavel is their Corp logo	Their new software is simple to use. We know legal	Indispensable; Credible

ValuePropInteractive QC: 647

NOTES:

Competitive Awareness Assessment

The **Competitive Awareness Questions** are designed to measure your project readiness in knowing the competition you face for your target market.

Armed with the concepts from this module your team should be able to pinpoint who the direct competitors are, what alternative choices are available, who might be a disruptor in the market and what your points of differentiation are.

Mark the statements you agree with in the open box to the right:

#	QUESTION	+	–
1	We know who else is playing within the landscape of our target market.	☐	
2	We have a good sense of who/what the marketplace disruptors are most likely to be.	☐	
3	Our team has a structure in place to track the competition and their moves.	☐	
4	Our team is unclear what messages and claims each competitor is making.		☐
5	We know and understand the symbols each competitor is employing in their messaging.	☐	
6	There is overlap between our value proposition and our competitors'.		☐
7	Our team knows how our target market views each direct competitor, alternative competitor, and disruptor.	☐	
8	Our team is clear on exactly who the target market of each competitor is.	☐	
9	We are uncertain which competitor claims are most damaging to us.		☐
10	Our team is crystal clear on what points of differentiation we bring to the market.	☐	
	Count the checks in each column:	☐	☐
	Subtract the total in the "–" column from the total in the "+" column to calculate your Competitive Awareness Score:	☐	

QC: 3649

The Four Question Areas introduced in the FlightPlan arise throughout the life of your project. Use them as a framework to identify and sort through any questions or situations that come up which may slow your progress toward your Go-to-Market goals. (Many will fit into more than one quadrant, or move from one to the next as you work through them.)

QC: 423

Issues to be resolved:	**Decisions** to be made:
Information Gaps to be filled:	**Know-How Gaps** to be filled:

Competition Worksheet

QC: 4143

Competitive Matrix

QC: 624

Their Strongest Market: Who do they serve most and best?

Their Greatest Strength: What differentiates them most in the minds of their customers?

Our Strength vs. Them: What I³ Value Proposition dimension is strongest against each competitor?

Direct Competitors

QC: 629

	THEIR STRONGEST MARKET	THEIR GREATEST STRENGTH	OUR GREATEST STRENGTH vs. THEM
Direct Competitor #1:			
Direct Competitor #2:			
Direct Competitor #3:			

Alternatives

QC: 631

	THEIR STRONGEST MARKET	THEIR GREATEST STRENGTH	OUR GREATEST STRENGTH vs. THEM
Alternative #1:			
Alternative #2:			

Disruptors

QC: 633

	THEIR STRONGEST MARKET	THEIR GREATEST STRENGTH	OUR GREATEST STRENGTH vs. THEM
Disruptor #1:			
Disruptor #2:			

Competitive Communications

QC: 645

Claims are assertions, usually characterized by a measurable factor, that sound like statements of fact, whether they're true or not.

Symbols are the images and metaphors used to communicate ideas companies want customers to associate with them.

Messages are emotional words communicated in terms of the products value proposition and broader details surrounding the product.

What are our...	How does this distinguish us from the competition?	How could this expose our weaknesses?
CLAIMS		
1.		
2.		
3.		
SYMBOLS		
1.		
2.		
3.		
MESSAGES		
1.		
2.		
3.		

Competitor #1:

QC: 647

	How strong are these versus us?	How do they hold up against the facts?	How is/could this be damaging to us?
CLAIMS			
1.			
2.			
3.			
SYMBOLS			
1.			
2.			
3.			
MESSAGES			
1.			
2.			
3.			

Competitor #2:

QC: 647

	How strong are these versus us?	How do they hold up against the facts?	How is/could this be damaging to us?
CLAIMS			
1.			
2.			
3.			
SYMBOLS			
1.			
2.			
3.			
MESSAGES			
1.			
2.			
3.			

FLIGHTPLAN | CUSTOMER | MARKET | COMPETITION | VALUE PROP | PRICING | MESSAGING | STRATEGY | PROGRAMS

Competitor #3:

QC: 647

	How strong are these versus us?	How do they hold up against the facts?	How is/could this be damaging to us?
CLAIMS			
1.			
2.			
3.			
SYMBOLS			
1.			
2.			
3.			
MESSAGES			
1.			
2.			
3.			

Value Prop

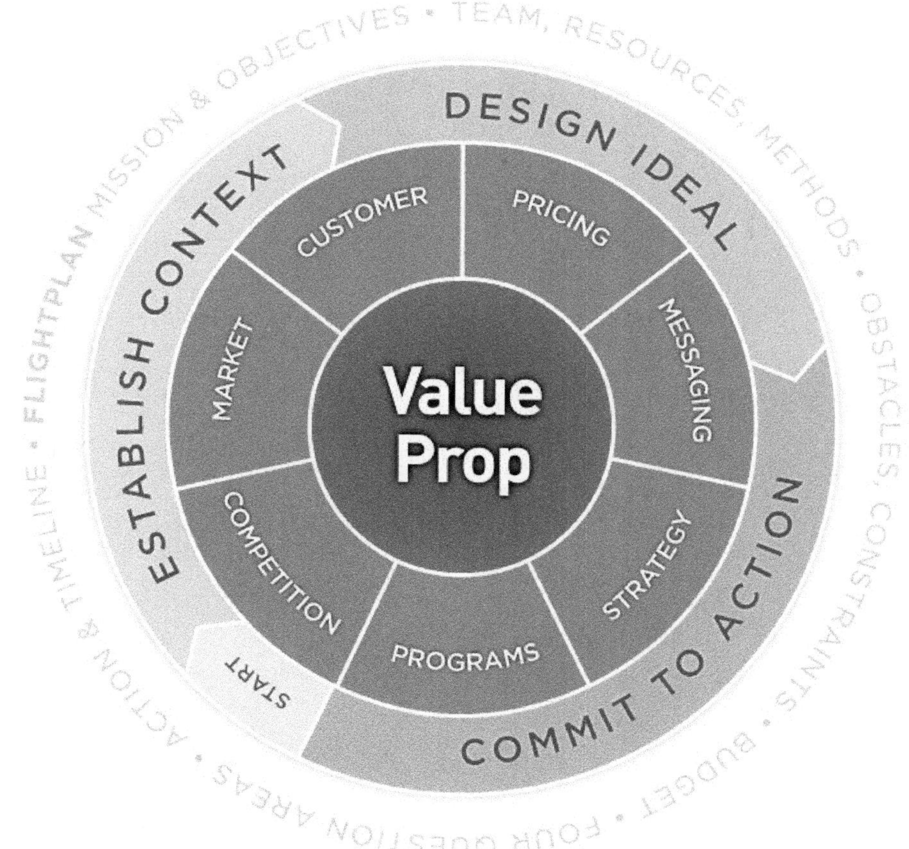

FLIGHTPLAN MISSION & OBJECTIVES • TEAM, RESOURCES, METHODS • OBSTACLES, CONSTRAINTS • BUDGET • FOUR QUESTION AREAS • ACTION & TIMELINE •
DESIGN IDEAL
ESTABLISH CONTEXT
COMMIT TO ACTION
START
CUSTOMER
PRICING
MESSAGING
STRATEGY
PROGRAMS
COMPETITION
MARKET
Value Prop

Start with I^3

QC: 5269

Don't "spin" or convince yourself that your product is differentiated if it isn't. A well thought-out "Sales Case" will ensure your product enters the marketplace with a strong messaging foundation.

If you build it, they will come.

We have probably all learned by now that this is just not true. Great – or even stellar – product features are not enough. Being better is not enough. Even being the best is not enough.

The imperative for today's companies is to build a stellar message to accompany your stellar product in the marketplace.

Your product cannot and will not **sell itself**, no matter how good it is. While marketers are trying to manage social, word-of-mouth, and other viral marketing techniques, these have less (but definite) relevance for business products and services and we'll see how later.

Start with I^3 Sales Cases

Additionally, your prospect is too busy to really study your offering to see relevant attributes that you know are great. Keeping in mind the realistic potential of the promises firms can reasonably make to target audiences, this part of the methodology builds out the messaging matrix of your new product offering – that is, it refines messaging, so that it becomes a powerful marketing and sales tool.

By translating your refined and dynamic Value Proposition into what we call "Sales Cases" for your direct sales teams, your product and its grounded message will enter the marketplace with a strong messaging foundation.

FLIGHTPLAN | CUSTOMER | MARKET | COMPETITION | VALUE PROP | PRICING | MESSAGING | STRATEGY | PROGRAMS

Simplified Sales Cases Model

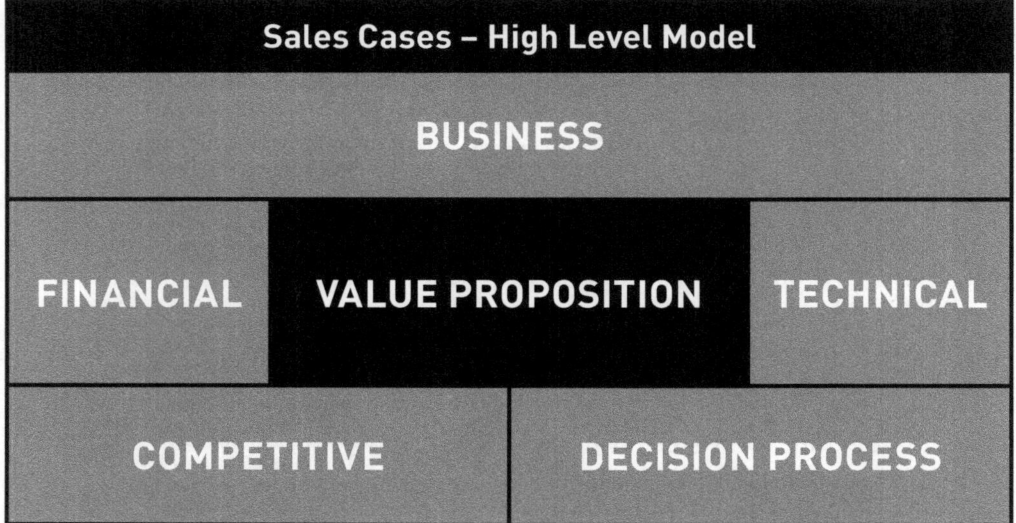

We will see how a simple and refined **I³ Value Proposition** describes your product's promises as an **Innovative**, **Indispensable**, and **Inspirational** solution. The Sales Cases draw on the I³ Value Proposition, providing sales professionals with a well-developed marketing message, targeted to the needs of specific customers, in the dimensions of decision making that organizations typically use to make purchases: namely, business, technical, financial, competitive, and overall decision cases.

Don't make the mistake of going to market without a polished messaging platform – one that flows from brand, positioning, and tagline to business focused cases as well. Take the time to understand why the product is valuable to prospects and make a clear case as to why the product is Innovative, Indispensable, and Inspirational.

QC: 5269

Definition: Value Proposition

- A **set of promises**, based on the capabilities and credibility of the **offering party** that help **prospective customers** understand the features and benefits of the offering and the **problems and challenges** they address.

ValuePropInteractive QC: 566

NOTES:

Start with the Truth

- Start with an honest, objective assessment of your offering, and work from there.
- Your team may be biased, so ask people outside your organization for feedback too.
- If you find you're at a competitive disadvantage, it's not the end of the line– gaps can be resolved.

ValuePropInteractive QC: 5340

NOTES:

Start with I^3

The I^3 Value Proposition describes the powerful connection your offering can have with your target customer.

- To what extent is your product innovative – **truly new** – *to your target audience*?
- To what extent is your product indispensable – **truly useful** – *to your target buyer*?
- To what extent is your product inspirational – **truly exciting** – *to your target market*?

ValuePropInteractive QC: 566

NOTES:

FLIGHTPLAN | CUSTOMER | MARKET | COMPETITION | VALUE PROP | PRICING | MESSAGING | STRATEGY | PROGRAMS

The Differentiation Dilemma

- CLAIMS
- E__________ C________ C______:

ValuePropInteractive

QC: 568

NOTES:

The Differentiation Dilemma

- **Product Superiority:**
  - This would be Intel and Apple for most of the last 10 years.
- **Customer Intimacy:**
  - In retail this is Nordstrom's –
  - In business services, this could be Bain or McKinsey.
  - In technology, there are less companies offering this today, but IBM has an historic reputation for "getting it done" for its customers.
- **Operational Excellence / Low Cost Provider:**
  - Think Wal-Mart and McDonalds in consumer, and Dell in computing[

ValuePropInteractive QC: 568

NOTES:

First - Discover Your Value

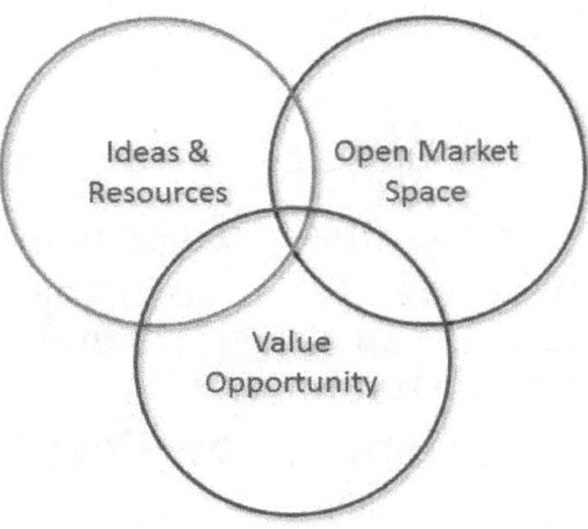

ValuePropInteractive

QC: 591

NOTES:

Discover Your Value

- Ideas and Resources
  - Your good idea
  - Your team
  - Intellectual property
  - Change the status quo
  - Unaddressed needs

ValuePropInteractive QC: 591

NOTES:

FLIGHTPLAN | CUSTOMER | MARKET | COMPETITION | VALUE PROP | PRICING | MESSAGING | STRATEGY | PROGRAMS

Discover Your Value

- Open Market Space
  - Understand your competitors
  - Know where the “open space” is in your target market
  - Customer’s greatest unaddressed needs
  - What solves their problem?
  - Who solves their problem

ValuePropInteractive

QC: 591

NOTES:

Discover Your Value

- Value Opportunity
  - Where can you add value for your potential customers?
  - Focus on space that competitors aren't crowding… yet.

ValuePropInteractive

QC: 591

NOTES:

Crafting a Value Proposition

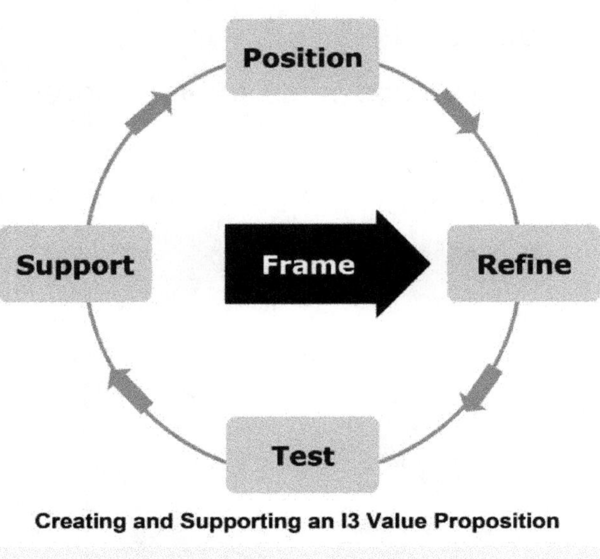

Creating and Supporting an I3 Value Proposition

ValuePropInteractive

QC: 571

NOTES:

Framing the Value Proposition

Frame your value proposition with a clear vision of your target market.

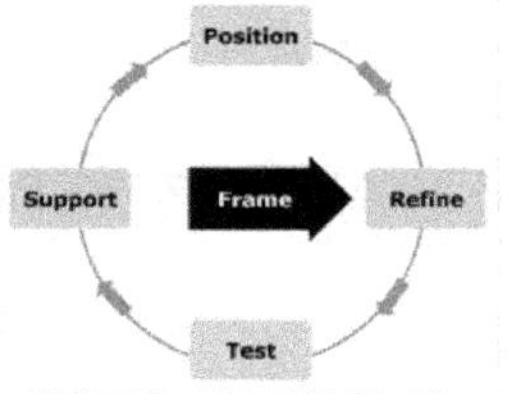

- Exactly whom are you targeting?
  - Will this be a company type (size, location, employee count), industry, culture (young and hip vs. old line and establishment), regional (US, international, or region within a country).
- More specifically, "framing" means developing a *30,000-foot view* of how your product is **Innovative, Indispensable, and Inspirational** ("I^3"), and doing so in terms that are understandable and exciting to your **specific target market**.

ValuePropInteractive

QC: 573

NOTES:

FLIGHTPLAN | CUSTOMER | MARKET | COMPETITION | VALUE PROP | PRICING | MESSAGING | STRATEGY | PROGRAMS

Framing: Innovative

Innovative – A New Twist

- To grasp your target customer's attention, your product must be offered as new, or at least offer a **significant new twist** on an existing product or product category.
- Mere line or "flavor" extensions are not typically new enough, from an I^3 Value point of view.

ValuePropInteractive

QC: 2678

NOTES:

Framing: Indispensable

- Who needs this product? Why is it useful?
- To what degree will it affect the daily operations of my target customers?
- To what degree would not having this have a significant **negative impact** on your target customer?
- Indispensability is not necessarily an implicit quality of innovative product offerings. Indispensable products live past the initial innovative stage:
  - They are not just passing fads.
  - Their utility is a persistent quality.
  - Indispensability is utility.

$$\text{Indispensability} = \frac{\text{(True Utility x Time)}}{\text{Ease of Integration}}$$

ValuePropInteractive QC: 2684

NOTES:

FLIGHTPLAN | CUSTOMER | MARKET | COMPETITION | VALUE PROP | PRICING | MESSAGING | STRATEGY | PROGRAMS

Framing: Inspirational

In short, the "WOW!" factor.

- Speaks primarily to design excellence – translating innovation and indispensability into something exciting.
- Inspiration and design excellence **target the knowledgeable observer** who looks at your product and says
  - *"Wow, it's incredible that they managed to do that."*
  - This means designing the product so well that it elicits admiration from a fellow practitioner of the art (a Ford engineer admiring a new Porsche, for example).

ValuePropInteractive QC: 2686

NOTES:

Refine the Offering Concept

- Your product or service
- Specific target market
- Benefits they want
- Differentiated features

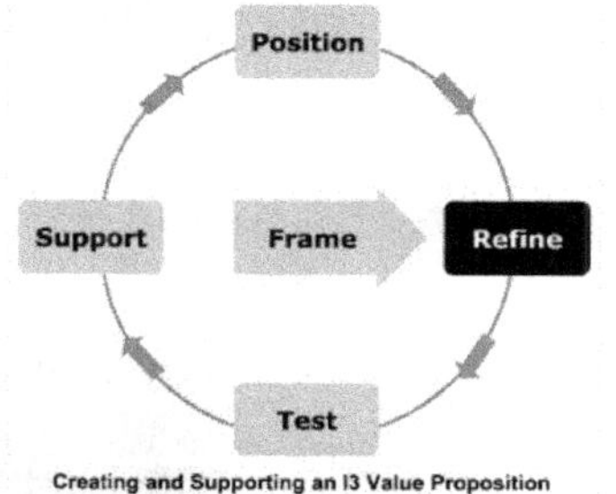

Creating and Supporting an I3 Value Proposition

ValuePropInteractive QC: 577

NOTES:

FLIGHTPLAN | CUSTOMER | MARKET | COMPETITION | **VALUE PROP** | PRICING | MESSAGING | STRATEGY | PROGRAMS

The Offering Concept Statement

- We offer OUR PRODUCT to SPECIFIC MARKET delivering BENEFITS THEY WANT through DIFFERENTIATED FEATURES.

We offer	to a	delivering	through
OUR PRODUCT	SPECIFIC MARKET	BENEFITS THEY WANT	DIFFERENTIATED FEATURES

ValuePropInteractive

QC: 577

NOTES:

Test the Value Proposition

Target Market: Describe your target market on at least three dimensions:		
Industry:	Company Size:	Geography:
I^3 Factors	These I3 Factors Will Matter to Target Market Because...	These I3 Factors Will NOT Matter to Target Market Because...
What we believe to be true about our Value Proposition.	*Focus on how receptive your target market will be to your Value Proposition's I3 dimensions.*	*It is important to call out why your target market might not be excited or moved by your Value Proposition's I3 dimensions.*
Innovative Factors:		
1 2 3		
Indispensable Factors:		
1 2 3		
Inspirational Factors:		
1 2 3		

ValuePropInteractive

QC: 2739

NOTES:

Support the Value Proposition:

- The Corporate Foundation
  - Credibility
  - Cost-Effectiveness
  - Capability

ValuePropInteractive

QC: 581

NOTES:

Corporate Foundation

- Credibility
  - Results delivered in the past
  - Experiences to support your reputation
  - Other references

ValuePropInteractive

QC: 2750

NOTES:

Corporate Foundation

- Cost-Effectiveness
  - Compare pricing to competitors'
  - ROI or perceived value for your customers
  - Other references

ValuePropInteractive QC: 2750

NOTES:

Corporate Foundation

- Capability
  - Demonstrate in your organization
  - Policies
  - Other references

ValuePropInteractive QC: 2750

NOTES:

FLIGHTPLAN | CUSTOMER | MARKET | COMPETITION | VALUE PROP | PRICING | MESSAGING | STRATEGY | PROGRAMS

Support the Value Proposition

Target Market: Describe your target market on at least three dimensions:		
Industry:	Company Size:	Geography:
Describe your Value Proposition's I3 Factors		
Innovative Factors	Indispensable Factors	Inspirational Factors
1 2 3	1 2 3	1 2 3
Corporate Foundation		
Credibility Story	Cost-Effectiveness Story	Capability Story
What in your company's past supports its unique ability to deliver the above I3 factors?	*What in your company's pricing and other supporting evidence points to your firm's unique ability to deliver the above I3 factors cost –effectively?*	*What in your company's resources (people, technology, partners, etc.) points to your firm's unique ability to deliver the above I3 factors?*

ValuePropInteractive

QC: 2750

NOTES:

Position the Value Proposition

- Positioning is a principle that manifests from your **target market's point of view.**
- It is how potential customers view a particular product offering in light of its competitors and based on a **particular set of meaningful attributes**.
- Positioning analysis and mapping takes into account not only your product offering and its competitors, but most importantly, those **attributes that most matter** to a specific group of customers.

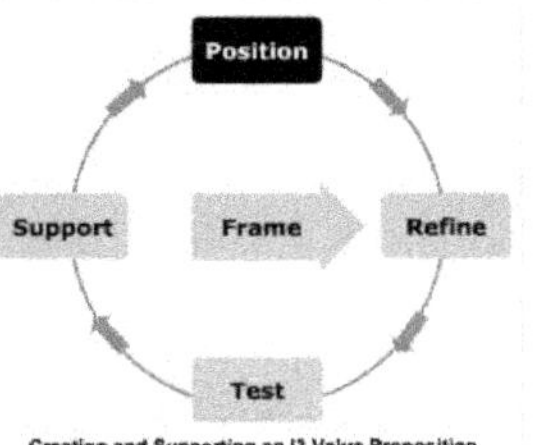

Creating and Supporting an I3 Value Proposition

ValuePropInteractive

QC: 583

NOTES:

Position the Value Proposition

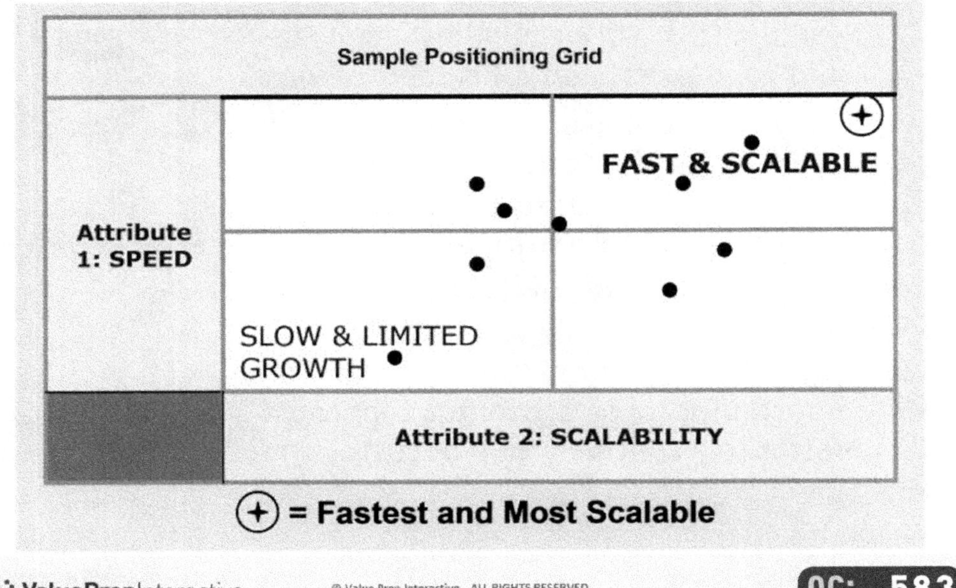

ValuePropInteractive

QC: 583

NOTES:

I^3 Recap Model

- Innovative
- Indispensable
- Inspirational

ValuePropInteractive

QC: 2690

NOTES:

FLIGHTPLAN | CUSTOMER | MARKET | COMPETITION | VALUE PROP | PRICING | MESSAGING | STRATEGY | PROGRAMS

I^3 Recap Model

- Core offering
- Core offering for specific market
- Offering for specific market, combined with something else

ValuePropInteractive

QC: 2690

NOTES:

Research and Validation

- Critical to test your Value Prop
- Resources
  - Customers
  - Employees
  - Industry experts and information sources
  - Internet

ValuePropInteractive

QC: 2736

NOTES:

Research and Validation

- Questions
  - How will your Offering Concept Statement be received?
  - Which competitors do you most resemble?
  - What features are most attractive to your prospects?
  - Others

QC: 2736

NOTES:

I^3 Value Proposition Assessment

The I^3 Value Proposition Assessment enables your team to assess where they think the team stands in terms of defining and designing your offering (Value Proposition).

Mark the statements you agree with in the open box to the right:

#	QUESTION	+	−
1	Prospects and current customers clearly understand our offering in "what's in it for them?" terms.		
2	Our product solves a very specific problem or issue.		
3	We have designed some exciting features into our offering.		
4	When you consider our whole offering (product and services), no one else in the market can offer what we offer.		
5	We often end up educating prospective buyers – and they end up choosing another vendor.		
6	Our product/service is not a short-term solution. It's actually useful to our customers over a long period of time.		
7	Prospects are crystal clear as to the financial benefits they would gain from our solution.		
8	Prospects often tell us we're like everyone else; They think they have already purchased or at least seen what we offer.		
9	Prospects and current customers see a clear difference and benefit in our offering over what they're using or doing now.		
10	Our competitors enjoy competing against us. Honestly, they don't really worry about us.		
11	Prospects usually get excited about the possibilities of using our product/service after we've demonstrated it for them.		
	Count the checks in each column:		
	Subtract the total in the "–" column from the total in the "+" column to calculate your Value Prop Assessment Score:		

QC: 3655

The Four Question Areas introduced in the FlightPlan arise throughout the life of your project. Use them as a framework to identify and sort through any questions or situations that come up which may slow your progress toward your Go-to-Market goals. (Many will fit into more than one quadrant, or move from one to the next as you work through them.)

QC: 423

Issues to be resolved:	Decisions to be made:
Information Gaps to be filled:	**Know-How Gaps** to be filled:

Value Prop Worksheet

QC: 4145

Discover Your Value

QC: 591

Discovering your value starts with an honest (sometimes brutal) assessment of what assets you have to work with. This does not mean that you are limited to what you can access today, but that gaps should be clear, and filled in before you go to market. The prerequisite to discovering your value is usually some concrete ideas, available talent, industry experience, and some kind of plan for what you want to offer and to whom.

Ideas and Resources

What "nugget" of an idea do we have?

In what industries does our team have deep experience and credibility?

Describe our personnel (skills, experiences, etc.):

What unique intellectual property do we have?
(Patents, trademarks, processes: all of these are ways you can create and deliver value to your target market.)

How would our offering change the status quo?

Open Market Space

QC: 591

Do we know where the "open space" is in our target market?

What needs are not being addressed by other venders, or perhaps even by our potential customers?

What would our potential buyers consider to solve their unaddressed problem?

Who would our potential buyers consider to solve their unaddressed problem?

Do we understand our competitors?

Value Opportunity

QC: 591

Where can we add value to our potential customers?

(by leveraging our resources and their unaddressed needs, and focusing on a space that competitors are not crowding – yet!)

Offering Concept Statement

QC: 577

After initially framing the value proposition for your target market, create a succinct but thorough offering concept statement outlining:

- The specific product or service you offer
- The market to whom you're offering your product
- The benefit derived from using your product
- Why your product is different

The identification of a target market begins with a simple hypothesis – the offering concept statement. Keep the statement concise and brief. Focus on breaking down the offering and its value to the simplest, most direct terms.

Think of the offering concept statement as a train of connected and inseparable ideas.

The Offering Concept Statement:

QC: 8148

WE OFFER	
	(your product)
TO	
	(a specific market)
DELIVERING	
	(benefits they want)
THROUGH	
	(differentiated features)

I^3 Recap Model

QC: 2690

The following model is an I^3 "prompter," designed to get you thinking about your offering in I^3 terms.

Think about what your offer is, in its most direct and simply descriptive terms.

QC: 8149	INNOVATIVE	INDISPENSABLE	INSPIRATIONAL
Core Offering Product/Service:	What we offer is new-new because…	What we offer is useful because…	What we offer is exciting because…
Core Offering for Specific Market Market in Focus:	What we offer is new to this market because…	What we offer is useful to this market because…	What we offer is exciting to this market because…
Offering for Specific Market, Combined with Something Else Partner or additional product or service:	What we offer, combined with [something else], is truly new to this market because…	What we offer, combined with [something else], is particularly useful for this market because…	What we offer, combined with [something else], is especially exciting to this market because…

Research and Validation

QC: 579

Test your Value Proposition and Offering Concept Statement as much as you possibly can, given your constraints (time, people, budget). Leverage your client base, employees who understand the industries you're in, Google, tradeshows, blogs, and every bit of news and information that flows around your market space.

Use the chart below to organize these resources around key questions that help clarify and validate your offering concept.

ASK...	CLIENTS	EMPLOYEES	INDUSTRY	INTERNET
How will your Offering Concept Statement be received?	*Describe it to a few trusted customers and find out!*			
Which of your competitors do you most resemble?				*Look up and chart competitors directly.*
What features are most attractive to your prospects?		*Avoid inside-out examination – it's too hard to be truly objective!*		
Add other questions and determine which of your "on-hand" resources could provide critical insights.				

Corporate Foundation

QC: 8150

You must create your firm's Corporate Foundation to ensure that customers view you as the correct vendor for the category of product you are offering. The Corporate Foundation includes three time-based dimensions or factors – credibility, cost-effectiveness, and capability.

Credibility

QC: 2750

There has to be a reason to believe that your company can deliver the promised value in your value proposition – credibility.

What results have we delivered for customers in the past?

What experiences can we reference that speak to our reputation?

What else can we reference that shows we are credible?

Cost-Effectiveness

QC: 2750

This dimension represents the hard-core present. This means pricing the product right, relative to its market and solution category.

How does our pricing compare to our competitors?

What is the Return on Investment (or "perceived value" for consumer offerings) on our product or service?

What else can we reference that shows we are cost-effective?

Capability

QC: 2750

While credibility looks to the past, capability points toward the future. Capability is what says, “We’re ready to serve you now, and we have the capacity to make and keep that promise.”

What in our organization can we point to that shows we can deliver?

What in our policies can we point to that shows we can deliver?

What else can we reference that shows we are capable?

Pricing

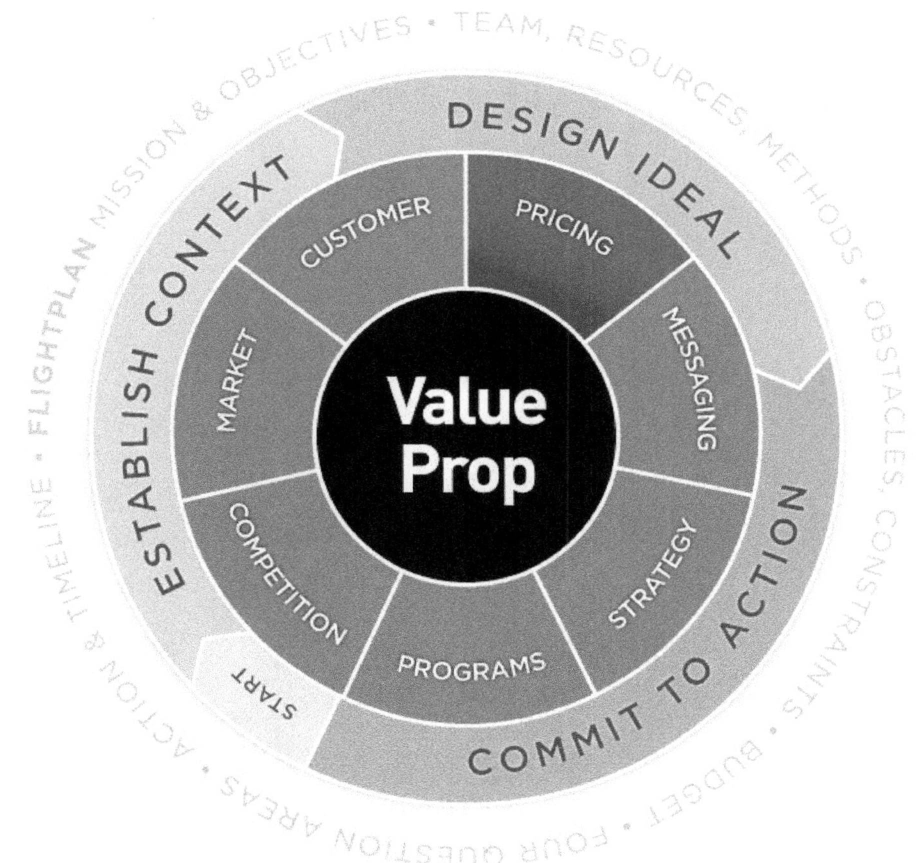
Value Prop
CUSTOMER
PRICING
MESSAGING
STRATEGY
PROGRAMS
COMPETITION
MARKET
ESTABLISH CONTEXT
DESIGN IDEAL
COMMIT TO ACTION
START
FLIGHTPLAN MISSION & OBJECTIVES • TEAM, RESOURCES, METHODS • OBSTACLES, CONSTRAINTS • BUDGET • FOUR QUESTION AREAS • ACTION & TIMELINE •

Volume, Velocity, and Value

QC: 6067

- Every part of your organization has to work toward sales transactions.
- Pricing establishes the revenue and profits from those transactions.
- Pricing determines the volume, velocity, and value of your sales.

Ask yourself, "What would be the likely impact on total sales and total profits, if we *lowered* our prices by 10%? What if we *raised* our prices by 10%?"

Every part of your organization – from product development, to manufacturing, to marketing and sales – is working toward one thing: sales transactions. Customer service supports those transactions, looking to create repeat and referral transactions.

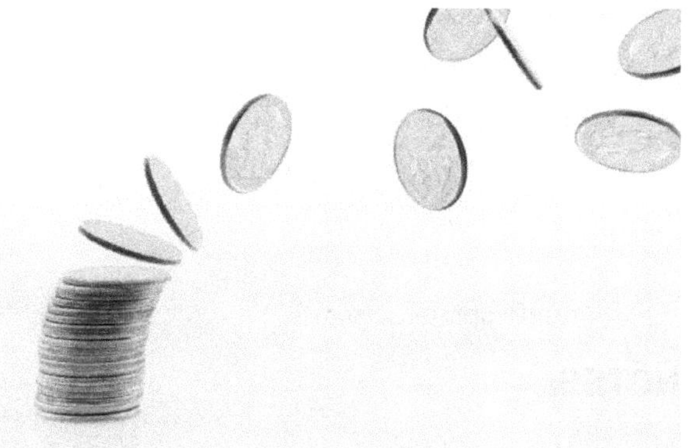

Pricing is the mechanism which establishes how a company generates revenue and profits from transactions. That is, pricing establishes what a company expects customers to be willing to exchange for your offering.

When you price correctly, your revenue stream will be as profitable as possible. Set the price too low, and you are exchanging margin (and total profitability) for volume; too high, and you may limit or throttle sales altogether.

Therefore, pricing determines the volume, velocity, and value of your sales.

- **Volume:** The total amount of sales revenue generated by an offering. This can also be seen as potential share of a given market realized by the offering.
- **Velocity:** The speed with which sales transactions take place. This can be the speed of transaction growth between time periods (i.e., month to month growth), as well as the typical "sales cycle" for transactions.
- **Value:** The profitability of transactions at a given price point. Marginal revenue and marginal profits (from microeconomics, see article) is largely a function of optimal pricing.

FLIGHTPLAN | CUSTOMER | MARKET | COMPETITION | VALUE PROP | PRICING | MESSAGING | STRATEGY | PROGRAMS

Pricing Strategies

- It is important to consider several influential elements that can affect your product price today and in the near future.
- Ignoring economic factors and the current market landscape can be detrimental to your launch.

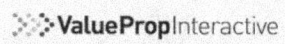

ValuePropInteractive

QC: 1239

NOTES:

Approaching Pricing

- You must develop an understanding of **demand** at each price point you're considering.
- You must know what your **costs** are, even if you are not basing your price on a cost-plus pricing model.
- You must research **competitors' pricing** and the prices of alternative products/solutions.
- You need to be aware of any **legal/regulatory** restrictions relevant to your product and its pricing.

ValuePropInteractive

QC: 6073

NOTES:

Pricing is a Strategic Choice

- Pricing plays into your business goals and your business persona.
  - High prices relative to the market will signal you as a luxury provider.
  - Ensure your pricing message is consistent with the rest of your business.
  - Business goals vary; be sure you're following the same strategy as the rest of the company.
- Determine which of the following you are after:
  - Gain market share
  - Stabilize market position
  - Minimize slide until the next product launch can stabilize revenues
  - Grow revenues
  - Grow profitability
  - Establish market position

ValuePropInteractive

QC: 6081

NOTES:

Customer Expectations

- Accustomed pricing in this category
- High-end competitor
- Low-end competitor
- Where you fit in

ValuePropInteractive

QC: 6073

NOTES:

FLIGHTPLAN | CUSTOMER | MARKET | COMPETITION | VALUE PROP | PRICING | MESSAGING | STRATEGY | PROGRAMS

Some Pricing Models

- **Cost-Plus Pricing** – Pricing from the bottom up. The price is set by using the production cost PLUS a profit.
  - *Example: cost + 40%*
- **Return Target Pricing** – The price is set in order to acquire a return-on-investment.

ValuePropInteractive QC: 6083

NOTES:

Some Pricing Models

- **Value-Based Pricing** – The price is set based on the customers' perceived value of product/service.
  - *Example: Consulting services or drug pricing, improved quality of life is worth more than the price of the actual ingredients in the medicine.*
- **Product Line Pricing** – The price is set incrementally based on differing levels of benefits from a range of products or services.
  - *Example: sofa with basic fabric $699, premium fabric $899, premium fabric and hand-tied springs $1199.*

ValuePropInteractive

QC: 6083

NOTES:

Some Pricing Models

- **Optional Extras / Add-On Pricing** – This applies to a current customer: capitalize on their spending by additional add-ons or extras, thereby increasing the overall sale.
  - *Example: Granite countertop is $X, honed finish is $X + Y, special edge treatments are $X + Z, honed finish with special edge treatment and sealed finish is $X + $Y +$Z + $Q.*
- **Captive Product Pricing** – Once a customer has purchased a product that requires complements or supplies, the customer is "captured" by having to replace accessories.
  - *Examples: ink cartridges for printers; blades for razors.*

ValuePropInteractive QC: 6083

NOTES:

Some Pricing Models

- **Bundled Pricing** – Sell a product with "package deals" combining several products at once (this is a smart way to move old stock and make happy customers simultaneously).
  - *Examples: warranties, internet phone service, or plane tickets and rental cars.*
- **Geographic Pricing** – The price goes up when the product is rare in one area (or shipping costs must be factored in); the price goes down when the product is local OR when local income cannot support a high price (but the need is great).
  - *Example: seafood, prime beef, and gasoline.*

ValuePropInteractive

QC: 6083

NOTES:

FLIGHTPLAN | CUSTOMER | MARKET | COMPETITION | VALUE PROP | PRICING | MESSAGING | STRATEGY | PROGRAMS

When you Revisit Pricing (which you should)

- **When to raise prices:** Once you've found your ideal price, the next big event everyone looks forward to is the day they can raise prices. It sounds much easier than it is.
- Choose your timing carefully; or conversely, do it consistently. And plan for the *after-effect*.
  - One option is to raise prices when the competition does.
    - Airlines are famous for this model.
    - One carrier bites the bullet, raises prices, and absorbs the ire of the flying public – and within hours or days, every other carrier has followed.
    - Consider what those increases are based on. For airlines, the trigger is frequently fuel prices.
  - What is it for your product?

ValuePropInteractive QC: 6100

NOTES:

When you Revisit Pricing (which you should)

- **How much?:** The next question to consider, after "When?" is "How Much?", and on which products? Everything all at once, or a series of incremental roll outs across your product assortment over a specified time period?
  - Does your target market have an expectation learned from your competitors?
  - The auto industry has established an expectation of price adjustments at the beginning of the new model year. Dry cleaners don't have the same luxury.

ValuePropInteractive QC: 6100

NOTES:

FLIGHTPLAN | CUSTOMER | MARKET | COMPETITION | VALUE PROP | PRICING | MESSAGING | STRATEGY | PROGRAMS

When you Revisit Pricing (which you should)

- **Discounts:** Price moves in both directions, and in certain circumstances you need to discount. Consider when those moments will be or to what audiences you will offer discounts.
- Some possibilities are employee discounts, trade discounts, or volume discounts.
- Others could be seasonal discounts, loyalty discounts, or price cuts to drive adoption or transactional velocity.
  - For every type of discount you offer, define the time period, frequency, and amount of the discount. Each will play into the overall strategy you are working toward.
  - Then, do the math. How much impact on overall sales and revenue do you forecast the discounts to have? Revisit your pricing model to assess if you can still achieve you business goals with the discount plans.

ValuePropInteractive QC: 6100

NOTES:

Pricing Positioning Principles

1. Pricing Positioning is a function of two connected but different **points of view**:
   – The Customer's
   – The Company's
2. Pricing Positioning is a function of **Opposing Dynamics** or Realities.
3. Pricing Positioning is **directional** and qualitative, not **definitive** and quantitative.

ValuePropInteractive QC: 9568

NOTES:

Pricing Positioning – Customer POV

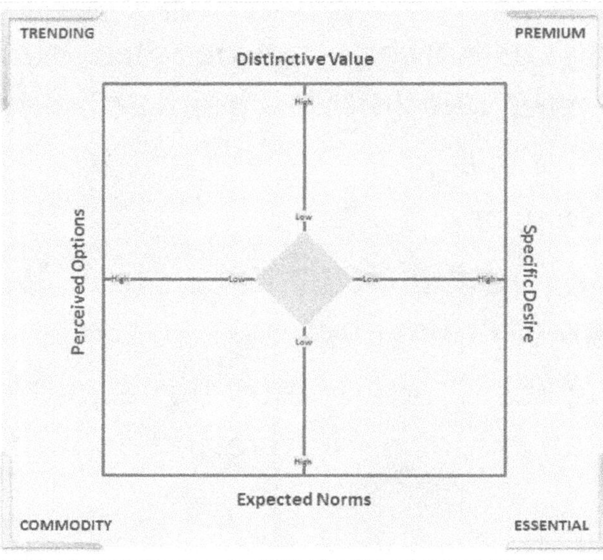

ValuePropInteractive

QC: 9568

NOTES:

Pricing Positioning – Customer POV

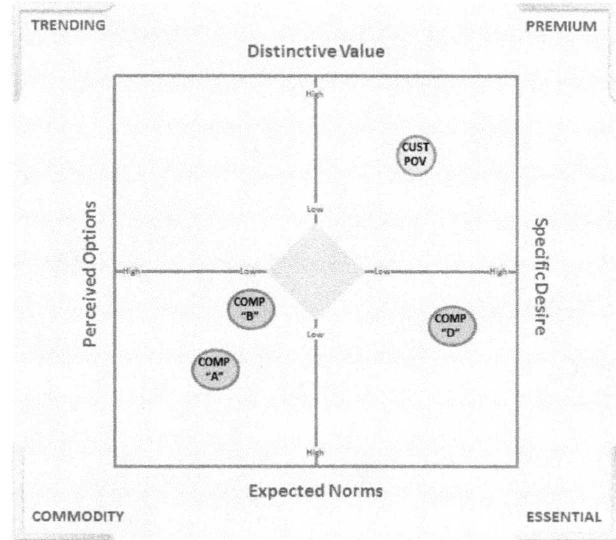

ValuePropInteractive QC: 9568

NOTES:

Pricing Positioning – Company POV

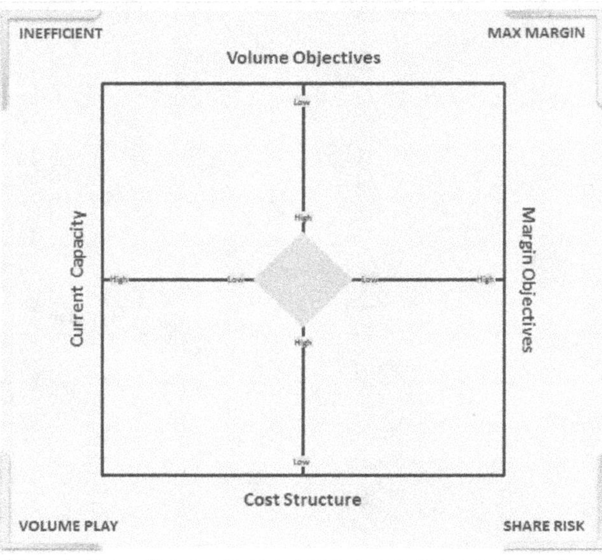

ValuePropInteractive

QC: 9568

NOTES:

Pricing Positioning – Combined Example

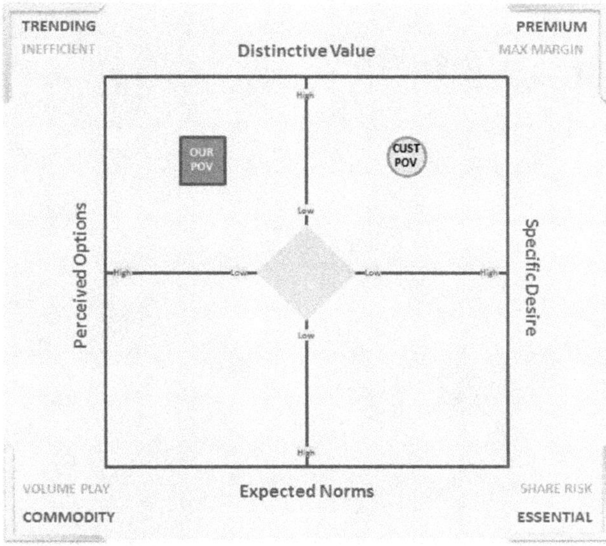

ValuePropInteractive

QC: 9568

NOTES:

Pricing Possibilities Assessment

The Pricing Possibilities Assessment enables your team to assess where they think the team stands in terms of defining and understanding your Pricing Possibilities – your options for pricing that are most consistent with your Value Proposition.

Mark the statements you agree with in the open box to the right:

#	QUESTION	+	–
1	We don't understand the kind of pricing our customers are used to.		
2	We know which competitor we "look" most like.		
3	We don't really have an easy "entry price point" for customers.		
4	We have a very clear idea of our current market share within our category.		
5	We have a clear pricing model.		
6	We know which competitor represents the high end of our market.		
7	We are clear as to how much contribution margin (operating profit) we want from this initiative.		
8	We don't know which competitor represents the low end.		
9	We are not sure the transactional speed (Velocity) we want for this initiative.		
10	We have crystal clear core pricing for our product/service.		
11	We have add-ons (products or services) that we offer as well.		
	Count the checks in each column:		
	Subtract the total in the "–" column from the total in the "+" column to calculate your Pricing Assessment Score:		

QC: 3663

FLIGHTPLAN | CUSTOMER | MARKET | COMPETITION | VALUE PROP | PRICING | MESSAGING | STRATEGY | PROGRAMS

The Four Question Areas introduced in the FlightPlan arise throughout the life of your project. Use them as a framework to identify and sort through any questions or situations that come up which may slow your progress toward your Go-to-Market goals. (Many will fit into more than one quadrant, or move from one to the next as you work through them.)

QC: 423

Issues to be resolved:	**Decisions** to be made:
Information Gaps to be filled:	**Know-How Gaps** to be filled:

Pricing Worksheet

QC: 4148

High Level Objectives

QC: 6067

When you price correctly, your revenue stream will be as profitable as possible. Set the price too low, and you are exchanging margin (and total profitability) for volume – too high, and you may limit or throttle sales.

What kind of market share ("volume") objectives do we have for this initiative?

What kind of growth ("velocity") objectives do we have for this initiative?

What kind of profitability ("value") objectives do we have for this initiative?

Customer Expectations

QC: 6073

As much as any factor regarding your value proposition, pricing establishes the competitive context for your product. Competitors' prices can be gleaned via a little research.

What kind of pricing are our customers used to in this product/service category?

Which competitor represents the high end? Which competitor represents the low end?

Which competitor does your company look most like? Are they high or low?

Pricing Options

QC: 6083

Once you've defined what your pricing strategy is going to accomplish for the organization, consider what your pricing will be based on. There are many varied pricing models, each designed to accommodate specific goals.

What is the core pricing for your product/service?

What are some add-ons (additional products or services) that could be included?

What are some ways to break up your offering to create an easier "entry point" for customers?

What else should you consider in finalizing your pricing?

What is your basic pricing model?

Messaging

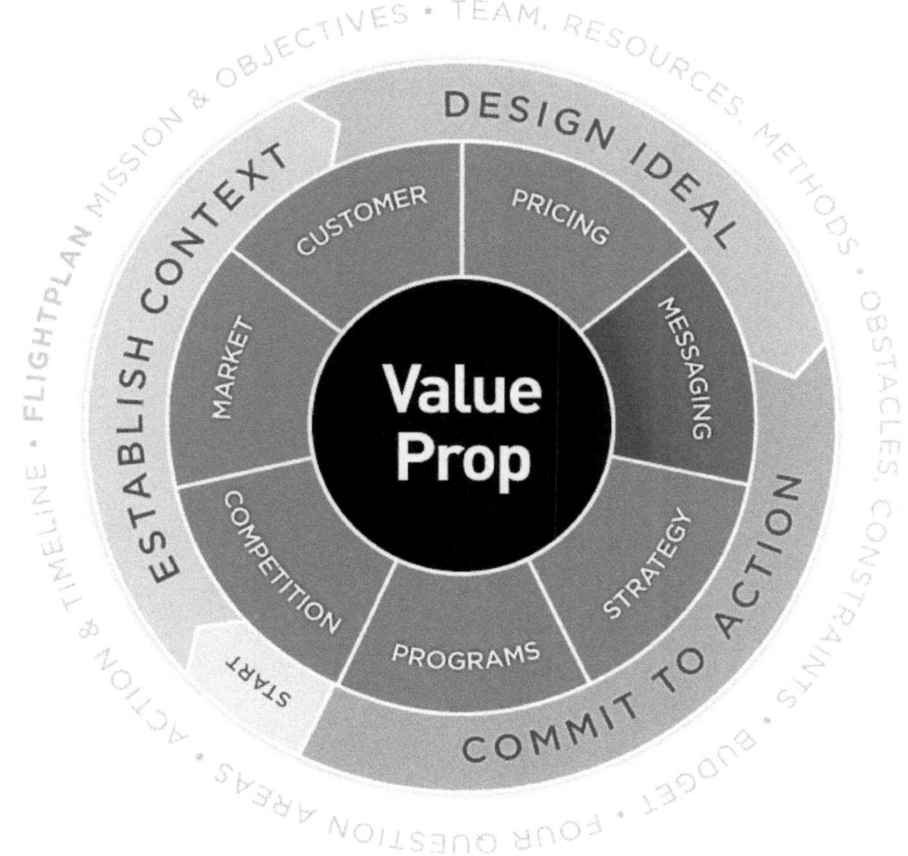
FLIGHTPLAN MISSION & OBJECTIVES • TEAM, RESOURCES, METHODS • OBSTACLES, CONSTRAINTS • BUDGET • FOUR QUESTION AREAS • ACTION & TIMELINE
DESIGN IDEAL
ESTABLISH CONTEXT
COMMIT TO ACTION
START
CUSTOMER
PRICING
MESSAGING
STRATEGY
PROGRAMS
COMPETITION
MARKET
Value Prop

FLIGHTPLAN | CUSTOMER | MARKET | COMPETITION | VALUE PROP | PRICING | MESSAGING | STRATEGY | PROGRAMS

Set Your Message Apart

- Excellent products and customer service don't cut it as differentiators anymore – now they're the minimum to get into the market at all.
- It's not enough to create value – you also have to be able to communicate that value to your prospective customer.
- Pulling the entire organization together around your message makes "disconnects" in quality, features, and support even more evident and urgent.

"Remarkable marketing is the art of building things worth noticing."

– Seth Godin, author, Purple Cow[i]

Product excellence and possessing stellar sales teams are "givens" in today's B2B world. Existing business literature and marketing "science" have created a global economy in which product and sales excellence are now considered the *baseline* or *"table stakes"* for business – the minimum for companies to enter the game. In a world where most players are aware of the baseline concepts for competition, new entrants must meet that baseline level of performance to simply close their first deal, or attract market interest of any kind.

Promises of excellent customer service or product excellence, by themselves, just don't cut it as differentiators anymore, even when they may in fact **be** a point of superiority in a product category. (For example, customers don't necessarily believe that vendor "A" is any better than vendor "B" in the areas of customer service and basic functionality... at least not at first.) These givens are the "infrastructure" of current business practices, which serves to elevate the importance of strategic messaging to a higher plane.

The entire organization and its culture must center upon the **message** of the company and its product. While at first blush, this might sound like a dangerous disregard for the "real" aspects of business value, such as quality, features, and support, it actually affirms these attributes. By pulling the entire organization together around the message the company wants to communicate, "disconnects" in quality, features, and support become even more evident and urgent. As champion NASCAR crew chief Ray Evernham put it, *"Everyone should feel as if his signature is on the finished product."*[ii]

What's Next?

So, what should the product or services vendor do? How do you make messaging – the communication of value to the marketplace – an *integrative* rather than simply a functional process? How do you build a go-to-market process and plan around messaging?

The Value Prop system describes an approach that centers your go-to-market process on a strategically designed message –a message that provides a business with a foundation that is critically different from simply focusing on product excellence, marketing programs, and sales execution. All of these elements are essential to business success, and an integrated messaging strategy can deliver leverage and increased power and effectiveness for each of these disciplines.

Message Platform

At the core, it is simple: a **messaging platform** provides the answers to the fundamental, philosophical business questions, such as:

- Why do we exist?
- Why should it matter to anyone?
- Whom does it help that we exist?
- What sets us apart from others like us?
- What is most important about what we do?

The answers, and how and when to deliver them, are slightly more complex.

[i] *Purple Cow*, Seth Godin, Penguin Books Ltd

[ii] Salter, Chuck. "Life in the Fast Lane," *FastCompany* Issue 18, September 1998. Page 175

Messaging Foundations

- Review Value Proposition and Offering Concept Statement
- Impact of and on company brand/identity
- Decision-makers
- Prepare specific talk tracks

ValuePropInteractive QC: 102

NOTES:

Set Your Message Apart

"Remarkable marketing is the art of building things worth noticing."

- – Seth Godin, author, *Purple Cow* **[i]**
- Excellent products and customer service don't cut it as differentiators anymore – now they're the minimum to get into the market at all.
- It's not enough to create value – you also have to be able to communicate that value to your prospective customer.
- Pulling the entire organization together around your message makes "disconnects" in quality, features, and support even more evident and urgent.

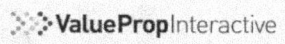

ValuePropInteractive QC: 382

NOTES:

Your Message Matters

"The average American receives more than 3,000 marketing messages a day."

– Dawn Hudson, former President and CEO Pepsi-Cola North America and CEO PepsiCo Foodservice

- Speed and message execution are also critical to success.
- Messaging is everywhere – **yours** and **your competitors'**.
- Success does not rest exclusively on the inherent quality of the product or service.

ValuePropInteractive QC: 697

NOTES:

FLIGHTPLAN | CUSTOMER | MARKET | COMPETITION | VALUE PROP | PRICING | MESSAGING | STRATEGY | PROGRAMS

Branding Strategy

- Branding is about presenting your organization and offering consistently, and getting people excited about it, both internally and externally.
- Your branding strategy should focus on what you want people to think, feel, and remember when they look at your product or service.
- The success of your branding strategy depends on understanding how your target customers think.

ValuePropInteractive QC: 108

NOTES:

Branding

- Review Claims/Symbols/Messages
- Aesthetics
- Name
- Tagline

ValuePropInteractive QC: 102

NOTES:

The Sales Cases

Yes – Messaging is for Salespeople Too!

"Exceptional sales professionals think like doctors – they diagnose problems before presenting solutions that could cure what ails their customers." – Jeff Thull, Inc. Magazine [i]

- What conversation scripts or "talk tracks" do your sales professionals use to close deals?
- Are you targeting your message based on specific prospects, or instead sending a generalized one-size-fits-all marketing message?
- Have you explicitly mapped out marketing messages and I^3 Value Propositions for the key conversations that take place in selling situations?
- Is your sales force prepared with a powerful overall messaging strategy?

ValuePropInteractive QC: 101

NOTES:

The Sales Cases

- ***The Business Case*** considers your prospect's mission, and the issues and processes they are trying to resolve, enhance, or enable.
- ***The Technical Case*** takes into account your prospect's ability to **absorb** your offering.
- ***The Financial Case*** analyzes a prospect's financial targets, thresholds, and expectations for purchases.
- ***The Competitive Case*** examines the strengths and weaknesses of your organization against the **landscape of options** your customer is looking at.
- ***The Decision Case*** defines how the selling organization works with clients to enable them to make informed decisions regarding the solution or product they are considering.

ValuePropInteractive QC: 2780

NOTES:

The Sales Cases

- Business Case
  - Mission Alignment
  - Endgame Alignment
  - ROI (Executive Level) Alignment
  - Vendor Lock-In Alignment

ValuePropInteractive QC: 103

NOTES:

The Sales Cases

- Financial Case
  - ROI (Deep Case) Alignment
  - Total Cost of Ownership Alignment
  - Terms Alignment
  - "RONI" Case

ValuePropInteractive QC: 104

NOTES:

FLIGHTPLAN | CUSTOMER | MARKET | COMPETITION | VALUE PROP | PRICING | MESSAGING | STRATEGY | PROGRAMS

The Sales Cases

- Technical Case
  - Compatibility Alignment
  - Ease and Flexibility Alignment
  - Requirements Alignment
  - Talent Alignment

ValuePropInteractive

QC: 105

NOTES:

The Sales Cases

- Competitive Case
  - Align to Competition
  - Question the Criteria
  - Be Response Ready
  - Money Matters

ValuePropInteractive

QC: 106

NOTES:

The Sales Cases

- Decision Case
  - Certainty of Execution
  - Process Match
  - High Value Match
  - Fulfillment Assurance

ValuePropInteractive QC: 107

NOTES:

Message Stack Assessment

The Message Stack questions are designed to measure your project readiness in defining your messaging. Messaging is a critical piece that connects your value proposition to the minds fo the decision makers.

Armed with the concepts from this module your team should be able to create messages for decision makers, sales cases and branding. You should have been able to simplify your message so it is clear and easily absorbed.

Mark the statements you agree with in the open box to the right:

#	QUESTION	+	–
1	We know our offering clearly connects to our brand's current identity in the market.		
2	We have a sense of who the stakeholders are in the decision-making process for our customers.		
3	Our team has prepared specific talk tracks for the sales team.		
4	Our team is unclear if our company's brand detracts from this offering		
5	We know and understand how to speak to the value proposition of this offering.		
6	We are unclear on the direction to give the creative team.		
7	Our team has developed a tagline that resonates.		
8	Our team is clear on exactly what the ROI for our offering is to our customers.		
	Count the checks in each column:		
	Subtract the total in the "–" column from the total in the "+" column to calculate your Messaging Assesment Score:		

QC: 3676

The Four Question Areas introduced in the FlightPlan arise throughout the life of your project. Use them as a framework to identify and sort through any questions or situations that come up which may slow your progress toward your Go-to-Market goals. (Many will fit into more than one quadrant, or move from one to the next as you work through them.)

QC: 423

Issues to be resolved:	Decisions to be made:
Information Gaps to be filled:	**Know-How Gaps** to be filled:

Messaging Review Worksheet QC: 4151

Messaging is a critical piece that connects your Value Proposition to the minds of the decision makers. Armed with the concepts from this section, your team should be able to create messages for decision makers, sales cases, and branding, and simplify your message, so it is clear and easily absorbed.

Foundations QC: 701

What is the Offering Concept Statement or value proposition for this offering?

How does our offering clearly connect to our brand's current identity in the market?

How does our company's overall brand affect this specific offering?

Your specific offering implicitly connects to your company's identity. Are they consistent?

Tailor the Message

Who are the stakeholders in the "typical" decision-making process for our product/service? QC: 703

Know who will be in the room at each stage of the game, receiving and questioning your message. Will it be the financial authority on the deal? Is it end-users interacting with your installation team?

Our team needs the following support or resources to prepare specific talk tracks for the sales team: QC: 101

Most organizations arm their sales reps with collateral, product, and sales process training. Go deeper by developing conversational models for your reps to connect key value points to the prospect's needs.

Deliver the Message QC: 108

What do you want people to think about, feel, or remember in connection with your product or service?

What direction could we give the creative team for an ad campaign?

What are some of the aesthetic attributes of your product? Of your company?

What are the claims, symbols, and messages you're communicating to your prospects?
(Refer back to the Competitive Communications section in Competition.) QC: 645

What is the significance of your company/product name? How does it align with what your brand is trying to convey? QC: 109

What's the tagline?
It's not enough to have just a matter-of-fact, one sentence description. The goal of a tagline, properly engineered, is to have some element of memorability to it. QC: 111

The Sales Cases Worksheet

QC: 8378

Built on an effective and validated I³ Value Proposition, the Sales Cases begin where marketing collateral ends.

By digging deeper and mapping messaging connections for conversations examining the business, technical, financial, competitive, and decision process issues of your prospect, the Sales Cases provide sales teams with powerful messaging strategies for real-world sales situations.

QC: 2780

THE SALES CASES OUTLINE				
Business	**Financial**	**Technical**	**Competitive**	**Decision**
Mission	ROI-Deep	Compatibility	Align to Competition	Certainty of Execution
End-Game	TCO	Ease & Flexibility	Question the Criteria	Process Match
ROI-Exec	Terms	Requirements	Be Response Ready	High Value Match
Vendor Lock-In	"RONI"	Talent	Money Matters	Fulfillment Assurance
I³ Value Proposition Foundation				

NOTES:

Business Case

QC: 103

Mission Alignment

Discover or create genuine alignment based on what you offer and what your prospect needs. Allow the prospect to understand that your businesses accomplish compatible goals and objectives.

End-Game Alignment

Communicate how your organizations (yours and your prospect's) define ultimate success.

ROI (Executive Level) Alignment

Taking the time to gain knowledge of your prospect's ROI considerations allows your sales organization to position its ROI story in alignment with your target market.

Vendor Lock-In Alignment

Most companies view Vendor Lock-in as a negative factor. It's best to address it as part of the big-picture business case.

Financial Case

QC: 104

ROI (Deep Case) Alignment

Return on Investment is simply the required investments and time-period to realize a return on that investment. However, customers may ask the seller to prove the offering's ROI.

TCO Alignment

The total cost of ownership of your product has to take into consideration installation, training, support, upgrades, and other future costs.

Terms Alignment

A potential deal maker or deal breaker, terms involve the legal and delivery structures that must be negotiated to close the deal.

"RONI" Case

While certainly not a formal metric of any kind, Return on Not Investing (RONI) acts as a derivative of ROI and examines what the client organization might gain by not making a purchase.

Technical Case

QC: 105

Compatibility Alignment

Vendors must illustrate that their offering is compatible with their prospect's current system, or why the product is worth the investment and resulting change management challenges.

Ease & Flexibility Alignment

Products that appear too complex or a hassle to implement will often fall from consideration. This is, of course, a relative comparison – in the context of its category.

Requirements Alignment

Evaluate your offering's features and benefits in terms customer requirements – what your target market values. "Dig deep" to uncover which requirements are truly important to a specific prospect.

Talent Alignment

Articulate the skills, experiences, and headcount required to take advantage of your offering, and the amount of training necessary to implement it.

Competitive Case

QC: 106

Align to Competition

Think about the competitive landscape. To whom would you say you are comparable? To whom does your customer think you are comparable? Both answers say a great deal about you.

Question the Criteria

After getting a grip on who is in the game, determine what the game is all about. By what criteria will competitors be judged? Secondly, what criteria do you want customers to consider?

Be Response Ready

Know what your weak spots are in comparison to particular competitors – but put the spotlight on your strengths, in order to mitigate weaknesses.

Money Matters

It is critical that you understand the financial aspects of your competition. How do you stack up financially? How will you highlight your financial strengths, even if you are not the lowest cost provider?

Decision Case

QC: 107

Certainty of Execution

Give your client the confidence that you not only have the experience to deliver on your promises, but the capacity and time to act upon your guarantees.

Process Match

How will your organization collaborate with clients to make the evaluation, purchase, installation, and support work as promised? Are your internal policies and processes are aligned with theirs?

High Value Match

Find the single thing your prospect (and marketplace) has articulated as being of greatest importance in making a buying decision – and connect the solution, or the deal could be lost.

Fulfillment Assurance

Define the formal guarantees for your promises. It is crucial to identify what matters to the customer and communicate what your organization can stand behind to them.

Strategy

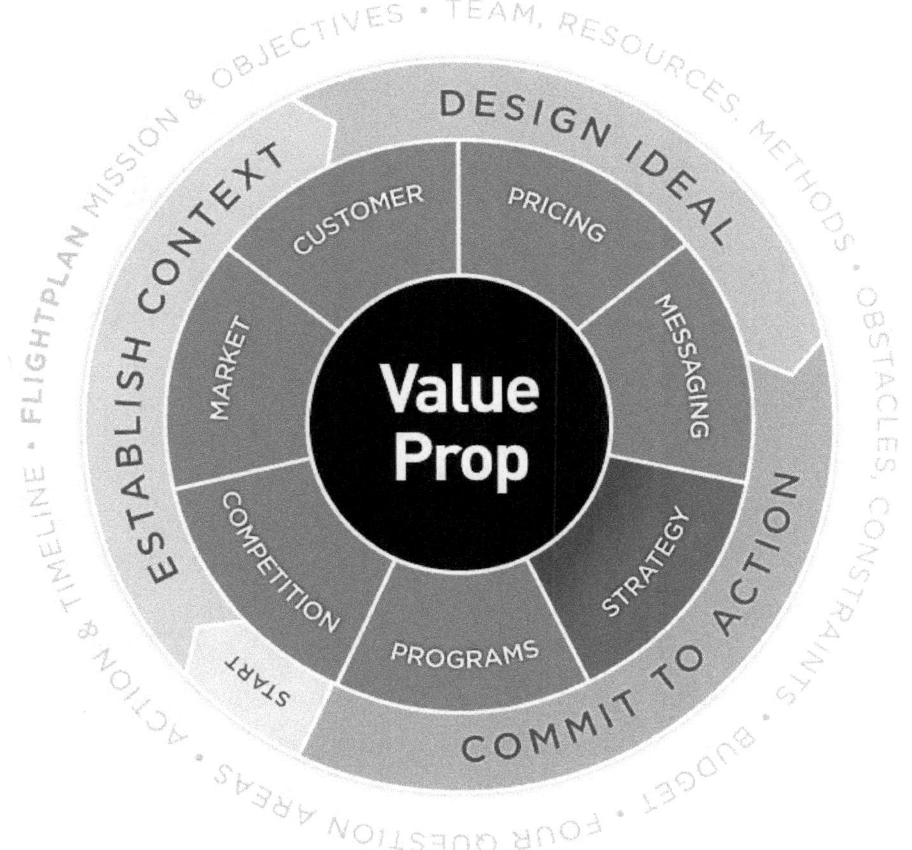
FLIGHTPLAN MISSION & OBJECTIVES • TEAM, RESOURCES, METHODS • OBSTACLES, CONSTRAINTS • BUDGET • FOUR QUESTION AREAS • ACTION & TIMELINE •
ESTABLISH CONTEXT
DESIGN IDEAL
COMMIT TO ACTION
START
CUSTOMER
PRICING
MESSAGING
STRATEGY
PROGRAMS
COMPETITION
MARKET
Value Prop

Your Market Entry Strategy QC: 3679

- Look for accelerating factors that can speed your market entry.
- Consider inertial factors that might inhibit or slow down your market entry.
- Determine the best market entry point for your company/offering.

Choosing the quickest path with the highest *probability of success* is one crucial element of your Market Entry Strategy. This is not to be confused with the *highest possibility of return*. If these two options are the same, you are in the best of all worlds – a veritable "success hot zone." Bear in mind that the Market Entry Strategy is not about gambling or luck, but preparation, rigorous self-assessment, and careful execution.

Early stage or venture-funded companies must keep this in mind, principally considering their limited time to go to market and succeed – typically, a very few short years. Unlike bigger players, small companies cannot continue to reboot repeatedly. "Success" has a very short-term component. *Will your firm gamble or invest?* However, even the largest companies have finite (albeit substantial) resources.

There are four major phases in the development of your Market Entry Strategy:

- **Define** your offering (this is the messaging stack of I³ Value Proposition and Sales Cases) for the Target Market
- **Examine** opportunities for Market Leverage and Accelerating and Inertial Factors
- **Articulate** your Market Entry Strategy
- **Match** the Market Entry Strategy against your I³ Value Proposition (this is a consistency test)

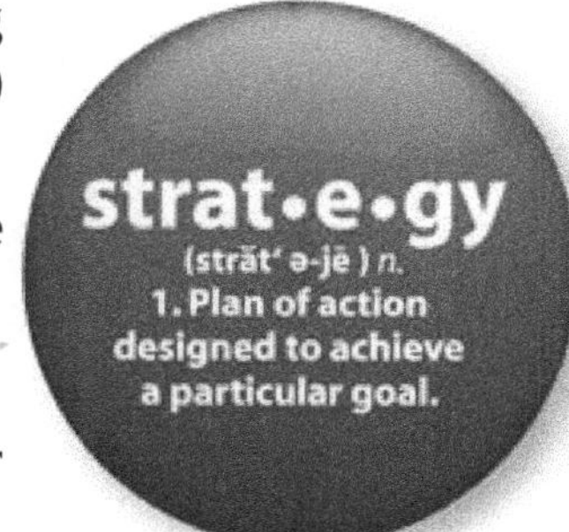

strat•e•gy
(străt' ə-jē) n.
1. Plan of action designed to achieve a particular goal.

Strategy is really all about decision making: it's a matter of taking a look at the options available to you and making a decision based on those options, based on your resources to act on those options, and based on the risk of doing or not doing this or that action.

It is all too often used as a word to describe inaction, i.e. *"They're strategizing,"* or *"We need to develop a strategy."* Many a *"let's-just-get-it-done"* kind of manager has often felt that whenever the strategy word comes up, it means to stop acting. There is some truth to that in business, where there can be "analysis paralysis."

However, in go-to-market – in taking that which you've carefully crafted as your Value Proposition to the marketplace, with the intent of winning – **strategy is all about making decisions for which actions to take, and it's that simple**.

Market Entry Strategy

- Look for accelerating factors that can speed your market entry.
- Consider inertial factors that might inhibit or slow down your market entry.
- Determine the best market entry point for your company/offering.

ValuePropInteractive QC: 3679

NOTES:

Market Entry Strategy

– Create Value

– Capture Value

– Communicate Value

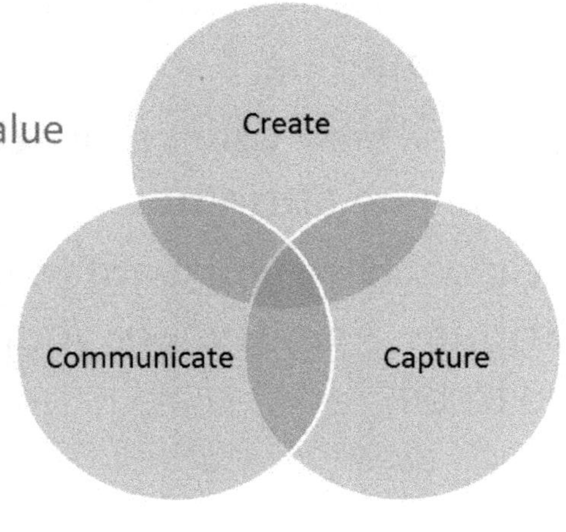

ValuePropInteractive

QC: 73

NOTES:

FLIGHTPLAN | CUSTOMER | MARKET | COMPETITION | VALUE PROP | PRICING | MESSAGING | STRATEGY | PROGRAMS

Review Positioning

- Review how well you deliver on two attributes of your offering.
- Review where your competition stands on those same attributes.
- Review where you want to be on those attributes – and where your customers want you to be.

ValuePropInteractive

QC: 76

NOTES:

Market Entry Strategy

- Getting to Market
  - Inertial factors
  - Accelerating factors
    - Core Assets / IP
    - Relationships
    - Trends / News

ValuePropInteractive

QC: 690

NOTES:

FLIGHTPLAN | CUSTOMER | MARKET | COMPETITION | VALUE PROP | PRICING | MESSAGING | STRATEGY | PROGRAMS

Market Entry Strategy

- Developing a Market Entry Strategy
  - Phase 1: Define your Offer for the Target Market
  - Phase 2: Market Leverage Opportunities
  - Phase 3: Potential Market Entry Points
  - Phase 4: Initial Market Entry Statement
  - Phase 5: Match Market Entry Strategy to your I^3 Value Proposition

ValuePropInteractive QC: 72

NOTES:

Phase 1: Define your Offer for the Target Market

The classic Four "P's" of marketing –

- Pricing
- Positioning
- Placement
- Product

ValuePropInteractive

QC: 668

NOTES:

FLIGHTPLAN | CUSTOMER | MARKET | COMPETITION | VALUE PROP | PRICING | MESSAGING | STRATEGY | PROGRAMS

Phase 2: Market Leverage Opportunities

Market Leverage Review worksheet	Accelerating or Inertial Factor?			
	How?	Why?	When?	Our Response?
Strategic Partners				
Channel Partners				
Patent or Trademark				
Investors				
Procurement Processes				
Other				

ValuePropInteractive

QC: 672

NOTES:

Phase 3: Determine Potential Market Entry Points

Review the options for your point of entry into the marketplace.

- Establish the key point of entry based on:
  - **Compatibility:** Determine the level of compatibility between your product offering and potential points of entry.
  - **Leverage:** What benefit will the point of entry bring your firm? Access to clients? Credibility? Function?
  - **Cost:** What type of explicit and implicit costs will your firm incur by choosing this particular point of entry?

ValuePropInteractive QC: 674

NOTES:

FLIGHTPLAN | CUSTOMER | MARKET | COMPETITION | VALUE PROP | PRICING | MESSAGING | STRATEGY | PROGRAMS

Phase 4: Create an Initial Market Entry Statement

Create a Market Entry Strategy Statement to summarize your plan succinctly.

For example:

We will enter the XYZ market by [define your specific approach or Market Leverage].

This can become:

We will enter the Financial Services Market by using Atlas Integrators (Strategic Partner) who are committed to our Proprietary 3D Market Forecasting software.

ValuePropInteractive QC: 676

NOTES:

Phase 5: Match your Market Entry Strategy to your I^3 Value Proposition

Test the statement developed in Phase 3:

"We will enter the Financial Services Market by using Atlas Integrators (Strategic Partner), who are committed to our Proprietary 3D Market Forecasting software,"

against all other assumptions, including the Competitive Matrix, the I^3 Value Proposition, and the Sales Cases.

- Does it hold up?

ValuePropInteractive QC: 680

NOTES:

Strategic Readiness Assessment

The **Strategic Readiness** questions are designed to measure your project readiness in defining and designing your winning strategy.

Armed with the concepts from this module your team should be able to defined an entry strategy, counter strategies to defend your position, how to leverage the market once initial traction is achieved and how to develop goals that align to those strategies.

Mark the statements you agree with in the open box to the right:

#	QUESTION	+	−
1	We know how we will enter the market.		
2	We have a good, solid counter-strategy in place.		
3	Our team knows which people and organizations can catapult our offering into the marketplace.		
4	Our team is unclear what feature is our "tip of the spear" to enter the market.		
5	We know and understand who our key initial buyers must be to gain traction in the market.		
6	We are unclear if there are marketplace factors that could slow our progress.		
7	Our team knows our market entry strategy is consistent with our value proposition.		
8	Our team is clear on exactly what metrics with which to track market entry success.		
9	We are uncertain if Sales is aligned with our goals.		
	Count the checks in each column:		
	Subtract the total in the "–" column from the total in the "+" column to calculate your Strategic Readiness Score:		

QC: 3682

The Four Question Areas introduced in the FlightPlan arise throughout the life of your project. Use them as a framework to identify and sort through any questions or situations that come up which may slow your progress toward your Go-to-Market goals. (Many will fit into more than one quadrant, or move from one to the next as you work through them.)

QC: 423

Issues to be resolved:	**Decisions** to be made:
Information Gaps to be filled:	**Know-How Gaps** to be filled:

Strategy Worksheet

QC: 4444

Value Proposition Strategy

QC: 73

Strategy is developed in three basic areas, and a value proposition is the intersection of these three distinct strategies. Your **value creation strategy** addresses how you intend to deliver benefit to your customers. Your **value capture strategy** is how you will get paid. Your **value communication strategy** is how you plan to get your message to your market.

How will you create value for our target market with our offering?

How will you capture value from our target market with our offering?

How will you communicate value to our target market for our offering?

Developing A Market Entry Strategy

Phase 1: Define Your Offer for the Target Market

QC: 668

What exactly does your product offer? What is the benefit it delivers, and in what timeframe? What does it cost? Break down your offering into discrete elements of features and supporting elements.

FLIGHTPLAN | CUSTOMER | MARKET | COMPETITION | VALUE PROP | PRICING | MESSAGING | STRATEGY | PROGRAMS

Phase 2: What are our Market Leverage Opportunities? QC: 672

Gain market leverage by "cracking the code" of which things, people, or organizations can catapult your product to market more quickly, and with stronger and deeper reach. Which factors may impede your ability to gain traction in the market?

ACCELERATING OR INERTIAL FACTOR?				
Who/What?	**How?**	**Why?**	**When?**	**Our Response?**
Strategic Partners Who?				
Channel Partners Who?				
Patents or Trademarks What?				
Investors Who?				
Procurement Processes What?				
Other Who/What?				

Phase 3: Select Market Entry Points

QC: 674

Review the options for your point of entry into the marketplace. Think in terms of how you can connect your offering to the market that needs to hear about it, and how to best get the product or service into their hands. Establish the key point of entry based on compatibility with your offering, leverage it would provide (access to clients? credibility? function?), and what it would cost your firm to select that point of entry.

	Entry Point	Compatibility	Leverage	Cost	How
1					
2					
3					

Phase 4: Create an Initial Market Entry Statement

QC: 676

Create a Market entry Strategy Statement to summarize your plan succinctly. For example: *We will enter the ____ market by [define your specific approach or market leverage].*

FLIGHTPLAN | CUSTOMER | MARKET | COMPETITION | VALUE PROP | PRICING | MESSAGING | STRATEGY | PROGRAMS

Phase 5: How well does our Market Entry Strategy match our I³ Value Proposition?

QC: 680

Review your Market Entry Strategy against the I³ Value Proposition. Do they make sense together and complement one another? Do your target market, competitors, and alternatives stay constant, or change because of your Market Entry Strategy? What revisions should you make?

Programs

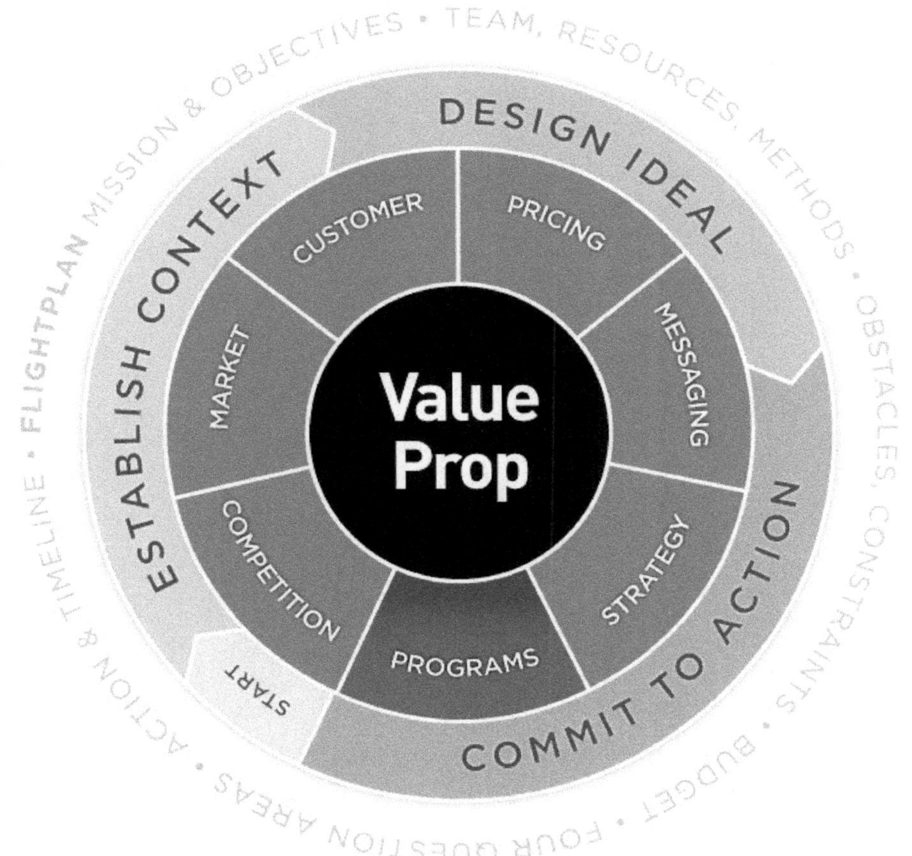
FLIGHTPLAN • MISSION & OBJECTIVES • TEAM, RESOURCES, METHODS • OBSTACLES, CONSTRAINTS • BUDGET • FOUR QUESTION AREAS • ACTION & TIMELINE •
ESTABLISH CONTEXT
DESIGN IDEAL
COMMIT TO ACTION
START
CUSTOMER
PRICING
MESSAGING
STRATEGY
PROGRAMS
COMPETITION
MARKET
Value Prop

From Strategy to Programs QC: 1309

- Use the strategic decisions you've made as the foundation to make sure that the execution is on point.
- Programs are about transforming your I^3 Value Proposition into a real, actionable message.
- Your Market Entry Program will map out the time, resources, and results that will be needed to bring your strategy to life.

"So, a brand needs to be more connected with a value-delivery system, and must not just be turned into a slogan or a name. Value is a ratio between what the buyer gets and what he gives up – that is, the ratio between benefits and costs."

– Dr. Philip Kotler[i]

Don't sit on it – TELL SOMEONE!

Sharpening your message and leveraging it to form a Market Entry Strategy is the necessary foundation for go-to-market action. So, what comes next?

Why, going to market, of course: delivering the message to those carefully selected buyers who will appreciate a specific promise of value – and pay for it.

In the following sections, we will look at several steps to operationalizing and validating your Market Entry Strategy. How to practically, quickly, and efficiently test the ideas and assumptions you have made about your offering and target market, by answering the only question that matters: *do your intended buyers buy?*

Get Go-To-Market Traction – or Die Trying

- How will you translate your long-term strategy into a winning program?
- How will you protect your message as you execute your strategy?
- How will you keep everyone accountable – every step of the way?

There is a still deeper story to be told. This is the part where the strategy leaves the office. Go-to-Market is about communicating, as carefully and thoughtfully as possible, messages from the strategic to the practical – owning the **messaging stream** for your offering.

Until now, the focus of the Method has put into place a strong set of "inspirational" objectives. This is typically when things begin to fall apart in the go-to-market process. Using the information gathered thus far, your challenge is to transform your I^3 Value Proposition and all associated material (assumptions, analysis, and several strategic decisions) into a real, actionable message – an *enduring* message that *"travels well to the very minds of your target buyers."*

The Road Map

The Market Entry Program transforms your strategy into a practical and results-oriented course. In short, your Market Entry Program provides a "road map" or "cook book" for an organization's **go-to-market activities**.

Keep in mind: *It is always about the **message**.* Each actionable plan, each Market Entry Program is always about the message – implicit in the I³ Value Proposition, explicit in the Sales Cases. In fact – **It is never *not* about the message.**

Your Market Entry Program brings to life the decisions that relate and rely upon the Market Entry Strategy, I³ Value Proposition, and the Sales Cases. Similar to the way in which the Sales Cases take the I³ Value Proposition and translate it into language that can be used when actually interacting with decision makers, your Market Entry Program will map out the time, resources, and results that will be needed to bring your strategy to life.

The Program will give you the necessary pieces to complete your FlightPlan – Objectives, Actions and Timeline, Budget, Resources and Talent required, as well as surfacing remaining Issues, Decisions to be made, and Information and Know-how gaps to be filled.

When Andersen Consulting changed its name, brand, and position, to Accenture in 2001, it faced an enormous challenge: changing the awareness of a global marketplace to successfully re-brand and re-position a market-leading company. With an aggressive $175 million global campaign that included print and TV advertisements, building ads, and sports sponsorships, along with 50,000 direct mail pieces to executives and other business leaders, the US brand awareness of the new name surpassed the old in just 90 days.[ii] The targeted combination and aggressively executed plan created the perfect combination to achieve measurable results.

Your firm may or may not have $175 million to commit to an advertising and brand development campaign. The objective, then, is to create a plan that fits your Market Entry Strategy.

[i] http://www.india-today.com/btoday/07111998/market.html – Dr. Philip Kotler is one of the world's foremost experts on the strategic practice of marketing and is the author of many influential books.

[ii] "SMM's Best of Sales and Marketing." Sales and Marketing Management, September 2001: 26-32.

Programs

- Use the strategic decisions you've made as the foundation to make sure that the execution is on point.
- Programs are about transforming your I^3 Value Proposition into a real, actionable message.
- Your Market Entry Program will map out the time, resources, and results that will be needed to bring your strategy to life.

ValuePropInteractive QC: 1309

NOTES:

Market Entry Program

- Baseline Elements
  - Define your market simply
  - Define your customer's universe
  - Make the connection
  - Understand word-of-mouth in your market
  - Review Branding and Corporate Identity Consistency

ValuePropInteractive QC: 765

NOTES:

Market Entry Program

- Establish Measurable Goals for Market Entry
  - Goals for this market/offering
  - Translate the message to prospects
  - Set specific and challenging goals

ValuePropInteractive

QC: 765

NOTES:

The Integrated Calendar

- The concept underlying the Integrated Calendar is to look at your message and Market Entry goals, and then match them to the **industry calendar** of your target market.
- These are the events, publications, and other **time-bound elements** that make up how your target market *flows* through a typical year.

ValuePropInteractive QC: 771

NOTES:

Marketing Communications

- – Creative/Visual Identity
- – Media
- – Social Media
- – Classic PR
- – Advertising
- – Promotions
- – Trade Shows
- – SEO/PPC

ValuePropInteractive QC: 126

NOTES:

Sales Program

- Integrating Sales and Marketing
  - Sales provide Marketing with data and insight
  - Marketing provide Sales with market intel
  - Systematic processes to ensure communication
  - Value the other's perspective
  - What remains to be done?

ValuePropInteractive QC: 390

NOTES:

Sales Program

- Direct Sales and Business Development
  - Strategic Account Opportunities
  - Ongoing Relationship Management
  - Lead Generation Programs
  - Marketing Materials / Collateral
  - Train Sales team to use the Sales Cases
  - Basic compensation model
  - What behaviors should it drive?

ValuePropInteractive QC: 80

NOTES:

Organizational Support Program

- Organizational Touch Points
  - Every interaction with customers matters
  - How is your operations team trained to support your strategy?
  - What remains to be done to train your operations team to support your strategy?

ValuePropInteractive QC: 813

NOTES:

Organizational Support Program

- Determining Policy/Promise Alignment
  - Internal and external policies affect your company's ability to deliver on the promises your Value Proposition makes

ValuePropInteractive QC: 815

NOTES:

Program and Action Assessment

The Program and Action questions are designed to measure your project readiness by practically, quickly and efficiently testing the ideas and assumptions you have made about your offering and target marketing.

Armed with the concepts from this module your team should be able to pinpoint who is buying and what factors most influenced their decision to buy from you.

Mark the statements you agree with in the open box to the right:

#	QUESTION	+	–
1	We know where our customers spend time.		
2	We have programs in place to support our sales team.		
3	Our team developed communications programs beyond the sales team.		
4	Our team is unclear who in the industry is most influential with our buyers.		
5	We know our company is internally aligned with the value proposition for this offering.		
6	There is systematic feedback built into the offering program.		
7	Our team has a clear schedule and budget for being in front of the customer.		
8	Our team is clear on who is responsible for the sales funnel.		
9	We are uncertain if our other offerings conflict with this offering.		
10	Our team is uncertain about the post-sell delivery process.		
	Count the checks in each column:		
	Subtract the total in the "–" column from the total in the "+" column to calculate your Program and Action Score:		

QC: 3687

The Four Question Areas introduced in the FlightPlan arise throughout the life of your project. Use them as a framework to identify and sort through any questions or situations that come up which may slow your progress toward your Go-to-Market goals. (Many will fit into more than one quadrant, or move from one to the next as you work through them.)

QC: 423

Issues to be resolved:	**Decisions** to be made:
Information Gaps to be filled:	**Know-How Gaps** to be filled:

Programs Worksheet

QC: 4155

Foundations

QC: 765

As the Market Entry Strategy (your overall direction and targets) is translated into the Market Entry Program (specific actions and tactics to fulfill the Strategy), there a few baseline or fundamental "must-haves" to keep in mind.

Define your market simply:

Define your market in terms of your product, and your product in terms of your market: do they match up?

Define your customer's universe:

How will we make the connection?

How does word-of-mouth work in our market?

What is our marketing budget?

Establish Measurable Goals for Market Entry

What are our organization's goals for this market? For this offering?

In what way will you translate the message to prospects in order to fulfill these high-level goals?

Why shouldn't our company garner [insert specific "challenging" number] new name accounts this year?

Specific Challenging Number: ________

What is keeping our firm from reaching [insert specific "challenging" number] dollars in revenues this year?

Specific Challenging Number: $________

Integration and Organizational Support QC: 4444

How does our branding support our Market Entry Strategy?

How is our sales team integrated into this strategy?

Does the marketing team reach out to the sales force for their input? Does the sales force share their opinions on new product introductions with Marketing?

What remains to be done to realize this type of integration?

How is our operations team trained to support our strategy?

Keep in mind, every interaction a potential or current customer has with your organization—not only during the sales process, but every "touch point" from first impressions, to delivery, to support down the road—affects the customers perception of your organization, and the likelihood of repeat business and referrals. QC: 81

What remains to be done to train our operations team to support our strategy?

Execution

QC: 79

How do you plan to communicate your Value Proposition to your target market? For each marketing activity below, consider what you will do, when it will be done, and the budget or other resources required to make it happen.

	What	When	Budget / Resources
Marketing Collateral QC: 128			
PR Campaign QC: 131			
Non-Web Advertising QC: 83			
Tradeshow Program QC: 775			
Social Media QC: 130			

	What	When	Budget / Resources
SEO QC: 806			
PPC / Online Advertising QC: 806			
Promotions (including joint promotions) QC: 84			
Direct Sales - Training QC: 797			
Direct Sales - Lead Generation QC: 773			
Other Marketing Activity QC: 129			

FLIGHTPLAN | CUSTOMER | MARKET | COMPETITION | VALUE PROP | PRICING | MESSAGING | STRATEGY | PROGRAMS

NOTES:

www.ingramcontent.com/pod-product-compliance
Lightning Source LLC
Chambersburg PA
CBHW061414210326
41598CB00035B/6208

* 9 7 8 0 9 8 1 9 1 2 6 2 2 *